IN THE CLASSROOM

Suggestions & Ideas for Beginning Teachers

Richard M. Trimble

UNIVERSITY PRESS OF AMERICA

Lanham • New York • London

Copyright © 1990 by
University Press of America®, Inc.
4720 Boston Way
Lanham, Maryland 20706

3 Henrietta Street
London WC2E 8LU England

Library of Congress Cataloging-in-Publication Data

Trimble, Richard M.
In the classroom : suggestions & ideas for beginning teachers
/ by Richard M. Trimble.
p.   cm.
1. Teaching.   2. Teaching—Aids and devices.
I. Title.
LB1025.2.T76   1990   371.1'02—dc20   90-34545 CIP

ISBN 0–8191–7815–2 (alk. paper)

 The paper used in this publication meets the minimum requirements of
American National Standard for Information Sciences—Permanence
of Paper for Printed Library Materials, ANSI Z39.48–1984.

Acknowledgements

Where does one learn the art of teaching? Unlike most crafts wherein you learn from a single mentor or from a manual or training course, teaching is learned from many sources and models. Books, education courses, colleagues, and even former teachers that you might have admired during your years of schooling all contribute to your teaching repertoire.

As a teacher, it is virtually impossible to recognize all those who helped me, over the course of a career, become what I am. As for the preparation of this book, I would like to thank a few people who have been instrumental. Cary D. McCormack has been my supervisor and served as a reader of this work. Andrew Long is a teaching and coaching colleague who also took his personal time to read and review this volume offering criticisms and corrections. Thanks also to Geneva Montgomery for reviewing the manuscript. Having sent out questionnaires to over one hundred high schools and elementary schools in New Jersey, I would also like to thank those who took their time to reply and offer ideas. They were credited in the text where their input appears. Thanks also Mrs. Susan McLean for editing and to Mrs. Christine Muly for typing the text, and to Bridget Patterson for the artwork.

As invaluable and unselfish as the help has been from those who have offered it, errors and misinterpretations inevitably exist. These are to be attributed to the author alone, with apologies to the reader.

Richard M. Trimble

TABLE OF CONTENTS

PART I

INTRODUCTION AND TEACHING PHILOSOPHY

"I teach what I know, and what
I don't know, I learn."

                    Gerbert
                    10th c. Humanist

"Try not to become a man of
success, but rather a man of value."

                    Albert Einstein

1

INTRODUCTION

Napolean Bonaparte once said, "We have only a short time for war." He was of course referring to generalship and the dynamics of leadership. Some would disagree, but certainly all careers have their peaks. If indeed we all have only a short time to make our mark, then herein lies my purpose -- to make the most of that short time and to try to extend it. I will try to impart to you some of the ideas and practices that I have learned, borrowed, or stumbled upon in my eighteen years of public school teaching.

I vividly remember my college education courses and teacher training. I questioned their practicality even then. Apparently things have not changed much at many institutions as my colleagues who work toward their post-graduate degrees in education agree that course content is largely philosophical and about as practical as trying to nail down smoke.

The thoughts contained in this book are designed to fill what I perceive as pragmatic need. Give our education majors something that they can bite into and use in their own classrooms. Give them ideas, practices, models and methods that have been tried. Tell them of those techniques that work and of those that do not. I am not an administrator nor do I have any desire to be one. I am a classroom teacher, and this book could have been written by any of the thousands of my colleagues.

Please excuse my bias toward secondary school teaching. This is my trade and my experience. Also, I am a history teacher; many of my ideas are geared toward that discipline. However, the subject of this book deals with such topics as classroom organization, student motivation, and effective lecturing, so I believe that there is something for everyone, whether a beginning teacher or a veteran of many years.

That being said, the education of a teacher must be on-going. Even the crusty old tweed-jacketed curmudgeon in front of the room needs to learn. The student of 1950 was different from the student of 1960, 1970, 1980 and so on. Accepting these differences, the teacher must change with his audience. How that change affects him and how well he adjusts determines how long he has "for war." Please do not think that I view my profession as a war, but no matter what I teach, no matter how often I have taught it before, the adrenalin still begins to pump after I have taken roll, laid out my notes and picked up my chalk. Napolean loved his profession, so do I and so must you in order to be good at it.

WHY BECOME A TEACHER?

Realize what you are getting into. The old adage that you will never get rich by working as a teacher is true for most of us. National surveys have shown that teaching is one of the professions that have the highest percentage of moonlighting for income supplementation. Surveys also have shown that teachers have one of the highest ratios of nervous breakdowns.

But before you change your major, consider the positive angles. Working with children can be frustrating, to be sure, and all too often your professional and public reputation will hang on the words and deeds of an adolescent or child, but more often teaching is truly satisfying and enjoyable. At the risk of a cliche', consider the impact you will be making on their lives. You still remember many of your teachers, do you not? Your students will remember you, too. What that remembrance will mean to them and what it will be is up to you. You may influence their careers, their college choice, their roles in the community and their roles as parents. What greater opportunity is there? We may not make anywhere near the money, but we have far more significant importance to society than the president of the bank, the chairman of the board, the doctor, the lawyer and the chief.

The rewards of teaching come in many forms -- tutoring a student through a course that you know he would have failed if you had not been there, helping a child with a career choice, being a sounding board for a child with personal problems, seeing the look on a child's face when you single him out for praise, coaching an athlete to perform above his expectation, or really "grabbing" the class with a lecture on something of keen interest. You never really get old in the profession if you work it right.

And then there are the vacations. You cannot beat the days off. However, in many cases your moonlighting chores or your coaching responsibilities will preclude an entire "day off." To take this a step further, consider that to get these days off, your teaching day and then the inevitable second job have forced you to

put in ten or twelve-hour days for most of the school
year. However, the alternative may be a nine-to-five
office job and that can be monotonous to be sure. And
then there are the summers, but realize that due to
finances most teachers cannot truly take the summer off.
Then again, what other professions allow you to
completely change your hours, work habits, and your
venue for two months?

        Despite the undisputed importance to society that
we do have, there are critics who will complain about
our pay or about our role, that should, in their eyes,
be subservient. All too often you may be the object of
barbs such as these, "I'm a taxpayer and I pay your
salary..." Or, "You teachers have it made; you rake in
the big bucks for a 180 - day work year, a seven-hour
day and the summer off." Although both statements have
their analytical truth, I pounce like a wounded lion
when these blasts are hurled my way. To the first, I
bite right back with, "Oh, you're the one who pays my
salary -- I've been looking for you. We've got some
serious negotiating to do!" Thus disarmed, the
belligerent will often mellow. To the second critic, I
assure him that most teachers, if they are the bread-
winners in their families, do not enjoy a seven-hour
day, but more often work a ten or twelve-hour day,
teaching, coaching, tutoring, preparing, correcting
work, or trekking off to a second or third job because
the basic occupation pays too little. Realize that a
teacher brings a lot home, both emotionally and
materially. Furthermore, in our business society with
its "perks" and built-in benefits, the average
college-trained executive works only 220 days out of the
year - forty more than you or I. Basically the
difference is the summer vacation, and I have already
established that most teachers in fact work in the
summer time. Challenge the critic with the idea that
teachers do not have a summer vacation; rather they are
laid off and must fend for themselves at jobs that often
pay minumum wage. Ask the critic to take two months off
from his job without pay!

        All told, your decision to enter the teaching
profession will bring you a great deal of satisfaction.
Some leave the field in frustration -- 41 per cent
according to a National Education Association study
reported in 1985 -- but many former teachers I have
spoken to find that they left the best years of their
professional lives behind.

A PHILOSOPHY OF TEACHING

I was asked at one point to summarize my philosophy of teaching. A lot of what I said then and what I feel now may be reflective of my love affair with my profession.

I believe that when one enters the teaching field, he commits himself to education in its most holistic sense. Just as there are many ways to learn, there are many ways to teach, and the more effective the incorporation of all of these methods and skills, the more effective the teacher.

A good teacher is not only a learned scholar, but also an on-going student. He must continually seek to deepen his knowledge of his teaching area. To do this, the teacher should attend any professional seminars he can. He must read; he should write and he must enroll in higher academic classes. I have a Masters Degree in European History and I know that I have used my graduate studies very directly in my own classroom.

The effective teacher must be an animated speaker. A noted author and scholar used to practice his gestures and lectures before a mirror to view himself as a student would and to test his choreography. Although perhaps over-done, this example serves to illustrate a point. Stuart Palonsky summed it all up when he titled his book on high school teaching, 900 Shows A Year.

The effective teacher must be a flexible technician in that he or she must use a variety of motivational approaches for the variety of students and classes he encounters. It is impossible to teach effectively in the identical fashion year after year.

The teacher should commit himself totally to his school. This comment is not intended in a sophomoric sense. I mean that extra-curricular involvement such as coaching and other non-academic participation will greatly enhance one's status within the student body, one's personal organization and motivational techniques, and one's effectiveness in the classroom. Circumstances aside, an eight-to-three teacher is simply not making the contribution he or she could be making.

Teaching is all too often seen as a second income or even a second job. This view is wrong. Aside from the commitments you make to your family and religion, your commitment to teaching must be of the

5

highest priority. More than any other profession, teaching affects the future. This principle must be believed, practiced, and then with realization, enjoyed.

Let me close my introductory comments with this piece by Kansas newsman Randy Attwood. It was reprinted in Ann Landers'column and says much about our profession.

AN OPEN LETTER TO NEW TEACHERS

Welcome!
We entrust to you our brats. We expect you to discipline them where we have not. But do it in a way that won't make us angry.

Keep our children entertained. They are bound to get restless. They watch a lot of television so they aren't very good at entertaining themselves. School bores them because they can't flip channels.

Some of us are ardently against abortion. Others of us are ardently pro-choice. Some of us demand school prayer. Others demand no school prayer. Some of us are Christians and hate atheists. Some of us are atheists and hate Christians. Please reinforce the correct moral views to our children who are in your care.

Feed our children well. We don't have time to give them breakfast at home so they are quite hungry when lunchtime rolls around.

We understand that teachers are human beings and have days when they are depressed, not feeling well and just plain have the blues. Never show that side of yourself to our children. We want them to believe the world is always a happy place. Smile.

Teach our children that America is always right, has always been right, and is the best place to live in the entire world and that now is the best time to be alive in the entire history of man. Of course we don't believe this stuff anymore ourselves, but we want our children to believe it. They will read enough negative things in the newspaper.

Remain in control at all times. Our children will yell at you. We will call you up on the phone and yell at you. We will go to the school and yell at the principal about you. Please stay calm. Someone has to.

Accept the great responsibility that has been given to you. If our children don't learn to read, it will be your fault. If they come out of high school having no idea what they want to do in life, it will be your fault. If they go to college and flunk out, it will be your fault. If they can't find a job, that will also be your fault.

Be perfect. Lord knows our children see enough imperfection in their homes. Somebody has to set an example.

And please don't gripe about money. Really now, you get three months of vacation away from the brats. We have to have them around all year long.

Yours truly,

The Parents

PART II

PERSONAL ORGANIZATION

"A teacher affects eternity; he can never know
where his influence stops."

anonymous

"Can you love anyone without making him work hard?
Can you do your best for anyone without
educating him?"

Confucius

9

PERSONAL ORGANIZATION

I never saw myself as a scatter-brained, disorganized person, but I look back now and admit that it took me at least five years of teaching until I became an organized professional. Still, each year something is added, discarded or changed that enhances my personal organization.

Let me start with the gradebook. The primary consideration here is that, in most states, this is a legal document and as such it can be subpoenaed; it is taken as gospel by administrators, and often it will be used as your word in absentia. If a parent, during the summer, questions a grade given by you in March, only the clarity of your gradebook stands between you and embarrassment. You may not even be present during said conference, so your documentation must speak for you. Also, your gradebook is often used by onlookers as an assessment of your professionalism. How well that sheaf of papers does all this is entirely up to you.

ORGANIZATION HINTS FOR THE GRADEBOOK

1. Always write entries in pencil. As a grade is changed, an assignment made up, or an error corrected, you will appreciate this.

2. Type the class roster - purely for the sake of clarity and neatness, the typing looks good.

3. Add in extra papers for each class. There is no eleventh commandment that says you can only have a certain number of pages per class. Add more so that you can record a variety of things - student identification numbers, homerooms, telephone numbers, grades, textbook numbers and so on. All these items are little things that will save you time if you must look them up. It always seems that the main office or the guidance people will send you a form requesting such data at the most inconvenient time. Perhaps, too, you may have to contact a student at home, this way you have all the necessary data at your fingertips.

4. Attendance listings: I have always found that it is easier to list absences in columnar form rather than calendrical format (see samples below). With the latter, you will write out all of the school days in a marking period, by date, across the top of the book's columns. To my mind, this method appears cramped and

10

scattered as you will record a student's absence or tardiness as it falls on a particular date. Similarly, you must record his test scores and homework points on those dates. As can be seen from the photocopies, the columnar system calls for you to record absences and lates as they arise, listing them in a separate set of column in the gradebook. Thus, at a glance you will be able to determine the number of absences and lates, rather than counting across the page.

To me, columnar format is clearly a neater, more organized approach. As for notations in the book, many schools have a required system, but if none is offered, here are a couple of simple examples.

sample columnar system:

Pd.6 U.S.HISTORY I	ATTENDANCE	HOMEWORK	QUIZZES	TESTS/REPORTS MAJOR GRADES
1 Aonson, Ari	L L L a	9 10 10 10 10 10	12 24 25	17 85 97
2 Cranwell, Laura	a a a L a L	9 10 10 5 7 7	20 21 0	87 85 90
3 Easton, Bill	a a a	5 9 10 7 10 7	21 20 20	75 77 78
4 Franklin, Tom	L	10 10 10 7 10 7	11 19 11	100 81 90
5 Harris, Leroy	a L a	5 10 10 7 10 10	19 17 5	71 81 57
6 Jenkins, Patty	L	10 9 10 9 10 9	22 25 17	88 73 70
7 Laswick, Troy	a a L	10 7 9 10 10 9	23 23 20	75 0 76
8 Martin, Lisa	a L	10 7 10 8 10 10	25 11 19	91 77 100
9 Meldwin, Bob	L			
10 North, Jamie	a	10 10 9 10 10 10	19 0 17	50 80 71
11 Rush, Anne	L L	7 9 10 10 10 10	21 12 21	89 95 85
12 Smith, William B.	a a a L	9 7 10 0 10 7	15 25 22	88 95 85
13 Smith, William S.	a L L	7 5 10 10 10 7	17 21 20	79 100 85
14 Vernich, Jennifer	a L	10 5 9 10 7 10	18 20 19	77 100 100
15 Walsh, Ricky	a L	7 10 7 10 7 9	25 11 15	83 90 90

Column legend (bottom, vertical):
EMP. 10 PTS.
CH. 15 10 PTS.
CH. 20 20 PTS.
CH. 21 10 PTS.
CH. 22 10 PTS.
V.N. EMPIRE 10 PTS.
FRENCH 25 PTS.
W. V. G. GUIDE 25 PTS.
ORALS 25 PTS.
TEST WARS / EXPLORERS 650
ORAL REP. w/5 BATTLES
TEST WAR II
BOOK REPORT

sample calendrical system:

Pd.6 U.S.HISTORY I																					
DATES:	15 16	17 18	21 22	23 24	28 29	30	1 2	5	6 7 8	9	12 13	14	15 16	19 20	21	22 23
Aonson, Ari	a	L			L	L			a		L					a
	7	25	10		97	10		25	95	25 10			83	10	10
Cranwell, Laura							a a	a			a	L			a
	9	20	10		87	10	21	85	0 5			90	7	7
Easton, Bill	a			a							a					L
	5	21	7		75	10	20	77	20 7			78	10	7
Franklin, Tom				L													L
	10	11	10		55	10	9	70	11 7			27	10	6
Harris, Leroy	a		L								a				
	5	16	10		100	10	17	81	5 7			90	10	7
Jenkins, Patty													L		
	10	21	9		91	10	25	80	17 9			57	10	10
Laswick, Troy				a a							L				
	10	23	7		88	9	25	73	19 10			70	10	9
Martin, Lisa	a L														
	10	15	7		75	10	11	0	20 8			71	10	10
~~Meldwin, Bob~~															
North, Jamie							a								
	10	19	9		90	9	0	77	17 12			100	10	7
Rush, Anne					L						L				
	7	21	9		90	10	12	80	21 10			91	10	7
Smith, William B.	a a		a								L				
	9	15	7		89	18	25	95	20 0			85	9	8
Smith, William S.					a						L				
	7	17	5		79	10	21	100	20 10			85	10	3
Vernich, Jennifer														a L	
	10	18	5		77	9	20	100	19 10			100	7	7
Walsh, Ricky	a										L				
	9	25	10		88	7	11	90	15 10			90	7	10

6	U.S.HISTORY I	121-09			Fall,1987		T.Lipman			
Aonson,Ari	9	A	B	B	c	C	B	B-	171	17880
Cranwell,Laura	9	B	D	D	c	B	B	c	172	16788
Easton,Bill	9	c	C	D	F	D	D	D+	159	12354
Franklin,Tom	10	D	D	D	F	F	D	D	187	15647
Harris,Leroy	9	A	A	B	A	A	B	A-	186	19000
Jenkins,Patty	9	A	B	B	c	B	B	B	183	18790
Laswick,Troy	10	c	B	B	C	D	c	C+	182	18905
Martin,Lisa	9	c	B	A	A	A	A	A-	181	13476
Meldwin,Bob	9	D	F	F	w/draw 2/7/87			F	179	14576
North,Jamie	9	A	B	B	c	c	B	B	160	19080
Rush,Anne	11	D	c	c	D	F	c	C-	161	12609
Smith,William B.	9	A	A	A	A	A	B	A	167	19453
Smith,William S.	9	D	B	c	c	c	B	C	184	19454
Vernich,Jennifer	9	c	c	F	c	D	c	C-	177	19678
Walsh,Ricky	9	c	B	c	B	B	c	B-	178	10098

Column headers (bottom, rotated): GRADE | MARKING PERIOD ① | MARKING ② PERIOD | MID-TERM | MARKING 3 RD PERIOD ③ | MARKING ④ PERIOD | FINAL EXAM | FINAL GRADE | TEXT BOOK NUMBER | STUDENT ID NUMBER

Gradebook suggestions, as advocated by:

MANASQUAN PUBLIC SCHOOLS
MANASQUAN, NEW JERSEY

Recording of Marking Period, Exam and Final Grades

Each class roster page, the first page of each class section, shall be filled out following the same format in every department at Manasquan High School.

1. Top of page shall indicate the period, course title, course number, name of instructor, semester and year.

2. Students' names are to be listed alphabetically last name first followed by first name and in parenthesis the grade in which student is presently enrolled. If a student enters or leaves the class, the appropriate entered or left date should be recorded next to the name.

3. Small columns (8) beginning with title "class" are to be marked as follows:

Column 1 - 1st marking period grade

Column 2 - 2nd marking period grade

Column 3 - Mid-term exam grade

Column 4 - 3rd marking period grade

Column 5 - 4th marking period grade

Column 6 - Final exam grade

Column 7 - Final grade

4. Remarks: Under this column the textbook number should be recorded.

5. Semester Courses: The only changes will be by column as follows:

Column 1 - 1st marking period grade

Column 2 - 2nd marking period grade

Column 3 - Final exam grade

Column 4 - Final grade

6. Please make use of the following symbols to indicate student attendance:

1. Absent from class: Square the date box

2. Late to class - under 10 minutes: Square the date box and slash.

3. Late to class - over 10 minutes: Square the date box and fill in slashed area.

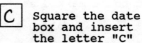

4. Cutting of class: ⌈C⌉ Square the date box and insert the letter "C"

7. All student activities/work (i.e. test, quiz, project, etc.) should be placed in the columns corresponding with the appropriate date assigned.

Homework and assignment listings: There are, to be sure, many systems that can be utilized to record student work and your school may require a particular schematic. However, after considerable trial and error, I have found a very workable system. First, consider your routine homework assignments to be graded as a base-ten of earnable points rather than a somewhat nebulous A or B. Even a numeral weight of 87 or 63 can be laborious when it comes to averaging them. You will certainly give at least ten homework assignments during a marking period. If a student earns 10 points with satisfactory work on each assignment, he will earn 100 points for his homework grade. This can be plugged nicely into the school's grading system. You will find it necessary to assess more or less than 10 points depending on the weight of a particular assignment, the student's effort, the work's lateness, or other penalty points for whatever reason. Just be sure that the ultimate total of "earnable points" is at least 100. In

16

most cases, this earnable total will exceed 100 points as more assignments are given and extra credit is added.

You have done your job by offering such a point total - now it is up to the student. If a given assignment is late, poorly done, or incomplete, then it should be assessed at five or seven points rather than the full 10. His returned work will thus have a fraction shown on it - 7/10 or 5/10 - rather than a letter or numerical grade. If the work was exceptional, it may read a 12/10. Very simply put, the student has the onus of responsibility put on him to earn the number of points he needs to pass. The criticism might be levied that this would reinforce only mediocre effort as once the student reaches 70 points, he is passing and then slacks off. All I can offer in response is that I have not found this to be the case. Furthermore, homework grades alone do not account for everything - there are tests, quizzes and reports also.

Record in your gradebook the set of points earned. It is a very easy task to simply total the points earned by the student at the time, especially if they are recorded in the gradebook in a specific area as can be seen in the columnar system I advocate. Totalling alleviates the cumbersome averaging and/or subjective leeway of an A- or B+ twilight zone. Furthermore, to keep the homeworks listed in a separate area of the page, quizzes in another and test in another area, makes the book look neater, reads more easily, and is more efficient in determining missed work on the student's part. Furthermore, it minimizes the tedious work of scanning the page to determine what grades should be averaged where and when. As a bit of an experiment, try totalling the homework grades in the two example gradebooks shown and assess which is easier and more efficient - the columnar system or the calendrical system.

THE IMPORTANCE OF FILES

No matter what subject you teach, you need a filing cabinet. As you come across more and more literature and materials that you may wish to keep, the filing system becomes a must.

What is kept in the personal files:
- ditto masters
- articles, essays and handouts
- term papers and materials from courses you are now taking in your major field of study

- transparencies for the overhead projector
- administrative directives and memos
- class projects that have been publicized
- home instruction grades and record sheets
- copies of memos sent by you
- exams
- letters
- observation reports
- maps and charts

Note that the above refers to personal files - things that pertain to you, cover you, and might be of necessity later. There is a second type of file - the personnel file.

The personnel files are more transitory, but they can be of great benefit.

I pass out all student work after grading and then collect it right back. The reasons I have for this are manifold. First, the student file serves as an important source for parents, the Guidance Office, and the administration who may wish to see a student's work first-hand. Second, by keeping the work, both the student and you have back-up documentation as to what a particular grade was or whether or not an assignment was done. The file eliminates the "I did that assignment, but you don't have any grade for me in your book" confrontation. Third, keeping a file containing all tests, quizzes, worksheets, and so forth, becomes a substantial aid to the student when mid-term or final exams roll around. I do allow the students to take their folders home on occasion, but with visible reluctance and with the understanding that if the file is lost and in the event a contest arises between the student and me as to a particular assignment, I automatically win the argument. Just before exams, I am often faced with the request to take their files home and I do grant their wish. I usually allow all work to be kept by the student one week after grades have been submitted to the office.

Let me qualify the above statement - I do not allow students to ever keep term papers and book reports. Over the years, these can too easily be copied by other students, especially if you assign specific books to be read year after year. Keep them; and keep them under lock and key.

I clean out the files one week after mid-terms and finals. And, by the way save the taxpayers' money by recycling the folders. Simply cover the old student's name with masking tape and use them again. The longevity of these files can be surprising.

The student file can be a depository for copies of deficiency reports, letters home, and personal data requests from the office. Sometimes this puts a bit of pressure on the student, knowing that his work is being scrutinized by others.

THE PARENT-CONTACT LOG

I started keeping this handy log after about ten years of teaching, and I did it as an academic inquiry. I was quite surprised at the sheer numbers of times I contacted people on a particular student. I decided to tabulate and record names and dates. The result has saved me considerable embrassment when a parent challenges me with "I never knew my child was failing."

Any letter home, any phone call to a parent, memo to Guidance or the office on a particular student is quickly jotted down in a notebook. I have found that I regularly make over 400 such contacts each school year. I do not believe that I am exceptional - most of us do this without ever realizing it.

Let me state here that I like to involve parents in the problems I may be having with a child. I have found too, that my reputation as one who "calls home" follows me. Parents love it. The administration appreciates it. Kids, many times, cringe. Be sure to include the praise-worthy memo or phone call also. This can be an excellent motivational supplement.

Berry and Glenn in their <u>Teaching For Excellence</u> even suggest a return to the old custom of home visitations by teachers to their students. I know of a least one kindergarten teacher who does this and it is positive for all involved. A telephone call can be just as effective. Certainly a commendable program, it may be somewhat impractical in terms of the number of students you might have and the time limitations all teachers face. Indeed, one teacher responsibility established by the Rochester, N.Y., educational renovation of 1987 was for each teacher to make regular contact with a client-list of 20 students and their families. If you have a large number of students assigned to you, a monthly newsletter home to parents can help. Write about assignments, homework, grades, and general concerns relevant to your class, its students, and their parents.

Once students reach high school, many parents tire of hovering over the child's homework each night, so under the rationalization of "He's old enough to do his own work," they abdicate responsibility. Keep the parent informed. Many like to cooperate once they know a problem exists.

To facilitate this aspect of your personal organization, have each child fill out a 3 x 5 card with the student's name, address, telephone number and parents name (if it is different) on the opening day of classes - before the students suspect anything on your part.

COPING WITH PAPERWORK

Paperwork - the albatross of modern civilization. We encounter it in running our own homes; we encounter it when we get sick, when we get well, when we pay our bills, and yes, when we educate our children. To cope with the inundation of paperwork, we should first look at a few basic facts. One, much of the paperwork emanates from two irritating sources: the need to cover oneself from future embarrassment and the need to justify the job of the person who is demanding the paperwork. Secondly, how much of it will ever be read?

There are ways to cope with all of the paperwork you will encounter as a teacher - from lesson plans to budget plans, from P.I.P.s to STEPS forms. First, photocopy everything and keep as much as possible. Obviously you have to cover yourself as well as your superior does. He will appreciate it when you have kept a copy of a submitted form that he has misplaced. You look good and he is quietly covered. Furthermore, it is surprising how redundant the data requested on the forms can be. Instead of rewriting, you can re-copy and save considerable time and effort. Secondly, do not be afraid to let students work on their clerical skills by giving them extra credit for typing book lists, ditto masters, courses of study updates, and so on. Thirdly, turn in the assigned paperwork as soon as possible. Not only does this endear you to the bureaucrats but also saves you from forgetting the particulars of an assigned report as it fades toward its due date. Fourth, turn the tables on the progenitors of paperwork by inundating them with replies, memos, blurbs, requests, copies and suggestions. In a sly way, such a turnabout makes you look good.

In the summer of 1984, John Lukacs, a professor of History at Chestnut Hill College, wrote an amusing, yet provocative article on the subject of bureaucracy and

20

paperwork in "U.S. News & World Report." I quote, "The inclination to administer, to standardize, to regulate, to reoganize, to define -- and therefore constrict -- personal activity and private choice is endemic in so-called private institutions, corporations, businesses as much as in public ones." This is very true of the teaching profession. Lukacs goes on to say that "the relatively uneducated and half-educated often express themselves in long words and surrealistic abstractions." Thus, some programs exist or are created that only serve to make some administrator look good. They may have little reality for the classroom teacher. Be that as it may, the paper plague is one of the many little headaches that goes with our job. Cope with the paperwork as best you can; we all share your plight.

WRITE IT DOWN

Every teacher is a supervisor. You have in your charge perhaps one hundred people. In the business sector, this means a top-salary and a prestigious job. For you as a teacher, it means one hundred different cases, problems, and ability levels. Unless you organize, you may find yourself out on a limb at times.

A student says that he turned in an assignment and you have no record of it - problem. A parent complains that you said that you would send home a test review sheet for his child and you forgot - problem. The vice-principal calls, asking about a three-copy student roster and you claim to have given it to a secretary two days ago - problem.

How you decide to organize and compensate for such dilemmas is best decided by you. I have seen and used file folders, stenographer books, file card boxes and so on. The bottom line is to write it down. Keep copies of memos sent out. This never fully solves all paper-related problems, but it helps minimize them. Writing things down saves embarrassment. Jot notes to yourself. This is not the pedantic practice of borderline senility; it makes good sense because, quite simply, some one hundred people depend on you.

Furthermore, both colleagues and students will then see you as a meticulous person and will admire you, the latter perhaps grudgingly, the former professionally.

Other techniques of recording your work have been mentioned earlier - the parent contact log, the student files, and the gradebook notations. A pocket memo book, a briefcase notebook, a desk clipboard - these, too, can

be used to assist your memory and accomplish the myriad
things asked you as a supervisor.

THE WEEKLY PLANNING GRAPH

In planning out your weekly lessons and
objectives, most schools will require the submitting of
weekly lesson plans. The format, content, and arrangement of these plans will be relative to your school
system. However these formal lesson plans do not always
lend themselves to the practicalities of day-to-day
teaching. I will deal with formal lesson plans later in
this book.

I offer the following chart that can be easily
adapted to daily lesson planning. It is nothing formal;
it need not be kept on file; it is for your personal
planning only. Set up a simple copy master and run off
enough for the number of weeks there are in a school
year, perhaps forty-three. As can be seen in the
attached sample, there are boxes for the days of the
week and for each period within the teaching day.
Simply label the classes in the appropriate box and jot
down what you want to teach to the class that day. Add
in reminders to yourself on what to mention or who to
see, points that were missed, homework to be collected,
and so on. This is a working lesson plan, not the kind
you would formally submit to the office.

I like to set this up on Sunday of each week,
jotting down things to make note of in class. I find
that I must add to each class box at the end of the day
or class, putting down what I must remember to do the
next day. This simple technique ensures that you "are
covered" for the next day - you know what you need and
you know what you intend to do. Furthermore, you will
remember a point that you might have missed or at what
point you stopped in your lesson coverage.

A colleague of mine, first grade teacher Adeline
McGreevey, utilizes the weekly planning graph in a
different way. She writes down reinforcement aids that
the parents can use in home study and then she sends
them home with the children at the beginning of each
week.

I have included copies of each type of planning
graph.

PD:				
PD:				
PD:				
PD:				
PD:				

HOMEWORK SHEET   GRADE 1   ADELINE B. MCCHEEVEY   WEEK OF: September 19, 1988

REINFORCEMENT OF DAILY CLASSROOM SKILLS

	MATH	READING WORDS	PHONICS	LANGUAGE	HANDWRITING	SPECIAL ASSIGNED HOMEWORK	SPELLING TEST WORDS
MONDAY	To add two numbers whose sum is 6 or less. *Study attached fact list.	Come not in at look	To decode CVC words at family. Ex. bat cat fat etc.	To write a telling sentence using capitals and periods.	Practice horizontal lines.	SOCIAL STUDIES OR SCIENCE SPECIAL PROJECT HOMEWORK DUE 9-22-88 SEE ATTACHED SHEET	1. here
TUESDAY	To write family of facts sums of 1, 2, and 3.	a good get	To decode CVC words an family. Ex. Can fan man etc.	To identify words that rhyme.	Practice vertical lines.	Math - To write family of facts 1, 2 and 3, (3) times each	2. she
WEDNESDAY	To write family of facts sums of 4 and 5.	you here's van	To decode CVC words ag family. Ex. bag rag tag et.	To listen to and follow oral directions.	Practice slant right lines	Math To write family of facts 4 and 5, (3) times each.	3. ball
THURSDAY	To write family of facts sums of 6.	he work said I	To decode CVC words ap family. Ex. Cap map nap et.	To retell a story about four related pictures.	Practice slant left lines.	STUDY FOR SPELLING TEST	4. can 5. cat 6. dig 7. run
FRIDAY	To know missing addends, Sums to 5. Ex. □+1=3	Review of above words.	To decode words with consonant digraph "ch". Ex. chop	To classify objects.	Practice spacing between letters.		8. play 9. with 10. one

*Study attached Word list.

Words should be studied every night.

TEST: FRIDAY

HANDLING PARENT CONFERENCES

To the first-year teacher especially, parent conferences can be frightening. I have seen veterans of five years enter into these contacts with trembling knees. Handling parent conferences need not be all that difficult.

First off, do not feel that every parent is coming at you with a loaded shotgun. The key, therefore, is to keep an open mind and a winning smile. Most parents are realistic about their child's academic failures (it is primarily on the athletic field and in the arts that we encounter true parental irrationality). In all probability, yours is not the only class that the child is failing. In fact, some parents are actually embarrassed by their offspring's performance. They are seeking your professional help and suggestions.

Secondly, prepare for the conference. Have your record book, the student's file and his most recent work. You will look bad if you cannot answer questions about why the student failed, what assignments were missed, or what his test grades were. Know exactly what went wrong before the question of why the child did so poorly is asked, as it always is.

Thirdly, anticipate questions. Aside from the ubiquitous ones just mentioned, there may be specific questions about the work, attitude, and attentiveness of the child. To stutter and fumble is unprofessional. You do not want your doctor to do this when you are inquiring about your physical health; parents want concrete answers when inquiring about their child's academic health.

Fourthly, offer definite suggestions. A parent conference is a waste of time if nothing substantive emerges from it. If the child is having problems with tests, offer to send home test review sheets prior to testing. If the problem is a lack of consistency on homework, offer to send home weekly assignment listings. If the problem is that the child lacks self-confidence, thank the parent for telling you and deal with the student one-on-one, praising him along the way.

The overwhelming majority of parent conferences you face will be designed to help failing students, not attack you. This being the case, welcome the parent conference. If however, you do sense an attack by a notoriously bellicose parent, obtain an ally. Call the student's counselor in to sit with you or hold the conference in the principal's office with him or her present. Bases will be covered and you will feel more secure this way.

PART III

CLASSROOM ORGANIZATION

"I am indebted to my parents for living, but
to my teachers for living well."

Alexander the Great

"You will make all kinds of mistakes, but as long
you are generous and true, and also fierce, you
cannot hurt the world or even seriously distress
her. She was made to be wooed and won by youth."

Winston Churchill

CLASSROOM ATMOSPHERE

The look of your classroom reflects your personality - it can be busy, philosophical, meticulously organized, sloppy and cluttered, vivacious, or bland. They come in all kinds, but the most important feature to remember is that it is where learning must take place, and as such you should devote some energies toward enhancing the learning process through a lively classroom atmosphere. Let the students know that you are organized and that you take pride in your classroom and that it is your office as a professional.

Make the room visually reflect your subject area. If you teach history, fill the walls with maps, photos, and charts. I once visited an impressive room decorated with old newspaper front pages. I have seen English rooms emblazoned with quotations and science rooms posted with charts in kaleidoscopic hues.

National Geographic magazine has excellent maps periodically offered during the year. Your librarian often receives posters dealing with various subjects. Professional publications and special interest periodicals often contain such materials as you may find useful. If you are still at a loss for posters, charts, and artwork, then assign it to your students to make some as a marking period project. Post the best work.

A focal point of student interest in some classrooms is the ANNOUNCEMENT BOARD. School and community events, bulletins, guidance news, athletic schedules, etc. may be posted here. Included also are humorous cartoons, anecdotes, photos, and the like.

Proper organization of the classroom can save you considerable time and effort also. A set of HOMEWORK ROSTERS placed on the wall containing student name, assignment, due date, and a check if the work was submitted will vividly show who is doing their work and who is not. Furthermore, it places the responsibility for making up missed work directly on the student as he or she always knows what assignment he has missed. The check should not be a grade; rather it should be a mere notation that something was turned in for that assignment. On the particular day an assignment is collected, have a student check off the collected work on the roster sheet. For all assignments coming after the initial collection, have the student submitting the work check it off. This saves you the effort. Include tests, quizzes, reports, and routine homework - everything done for a grade that the student is accountable for. Toward the end of the marking period, the homework roster saves the teacher considerable time when he or she is asked the inevitable and ubiquitous questions, "What do I owe?" or "What do I have to do to pass?" Point to the roster.

Take a section of your blackboard, mark it off, and use it as a regular listing of all upcoming work and due dates. Keep it updated and neat. This precludes the student challenge, "I didn't know about that assignment." Plus, if you teach many different classes it helps keep you organized in remembering the various dates and assignments.

STUDENT FILES form another segment of your classroom organization. I referred to this earlier. These student files, in coordination with the homework roster, can keep that potentially embarrassing challenge, "I did that work, but you lost it" from becoming reality. It covers you because if both of the aforementioned sources, as well as your gradebook have no record of the work, then the student has very little ground to stand on. Plus, the students appreciate all of this, as many of them honestly forget the work. Your classroom organization helps them out in a very real way.

HANDOUT TRAYS are another hint toward improving classroom organization. Nothing structurally fancy, these could be simple cardboard boxes, but place all spare dittos and handouts in such a tray embossed with the name and period of a particular class.

The aim of all this is to cut down on student demands on the instructors' time. Most of the demands are legitimate, but it is unfair to the rest of the class if you have to search through your lesson plans and gradebook to provide that individual student with the answer to his problem. Your lack of organization could rob precious class time. Thus, try to lay everything out to the students - assignments, missed work, handouts, etc. With all this data readily available to him, the onus of responsibility for obtaining such information is on him, not you. Properly organized, you can utilize class time more effectively and deal with real individual problems better.

SEATING CHARTS structure a class population. This may or may not be to your liking. With some classes, it may be necessary if the class is a discipline problem, but realize that just as your assigned seating cuts down on their group conversations, so does it inhibit their classroom participation to some degree. With larger classes, it helps the teacher to learn pupils names faster and it helps break up the talkative cliques that naturally form with such a large, captive population. If you teach high school or junior high and are assigned a homeroom, then the seating chart takes on near-Biblical importance. It expedites attendance-taking and fosters accuracy. This is seen as another plus for the big class, also.

It is a good practice to run off and pass out your classroom RULES AND REGULATIONS and explain them to all students on the first day of class. Some teachers do not like to be locked in to adhering to prescribed rules that may come back to haunt them, but I still feel that it is a good practice. A typed set of classroom rules that I use can be found below. I have used these for years and found them beneficial. Students like to know where they stand, what is expected of them, and what the teacher will require. The rules and procedures sheet defines this. Look over these classroom rules. There are some ideas that may need elaboration but most contain merit in and of themselves. Adapt them to your system and preferences.

On the first day of school, I always hand out a COURSE OUTLINE discussing what material will be covered in the course. Together, the rules sheet and course outline give the students a fairly well-rounded idea of what they are in for. Furthermore, many school administrations require, or at least recommend such practices. I ask that the student keep these sheets in their notebooks, not that they become the "Holy Grail," but that they may simply be referred to as needs dictate. The course outline may help to organize their thoughts and study when it comes to exam time.

STUDENT RESPONSIBILITIES & GENERAL INFORMATION

A) Attendance: School policy & possible failure/
                  competency test procedures.
                  Lateness is not permitted - get a
                  note before coming in room.

B) Note-Taking: A MUST as the bulk of my classwork
                  is lecture/discussion. Notebooks
                  are checked for grade. Keep all
                  dittos; check ditto tray. If absent
                  get notes from reliable classmate.
                  If absent for extended time, get
                  notes carbon copied from classmate.

C) Homework: Each homework is worth 10-15 points
                  toward your "homework grade." All
                  assignments are posted on side
                  blackboard. All work that you have
                  turned in is checked of on roster in
                  front-refer to this for status &
                  missing work.

                  HOMEWORK CAN MAKE OR BREAK YOU!

D) Tests: Given about every 2 - 4 weeks
                  Major grades 50% essays - I look for
                  organized, detailed essays.

E) Quizzes: Usually announced, but not always.
                  Each quiz is graded as a portion of
                  your whole quiz grade; i.e., quizzes
                  are not counted individually.

F) Required Work: Each of my classes has as required
                  work:
                      Book Report
                      Major Paper
                      FINAL EXAM
                  Note that each student MUST TAKE
                  FINAL EXAM
                  Note that failure of one marking
                  period necessitates the passing of
                  the final exam. Book reviews - 1,000
                  words: summary, critique, value.

G) Make-Up Work: It is the student's responsibility
                     to find out what was missed and to
                     make it up. One week is all that is
                     allowed for make-up work. Note that
                     end-of-marking-period deadlines may
                     shorten the one week period.

H) Grade Computation: Based on average of 3 - 6 "major
                     grades" such as test, written
                     work, cumulative quizzes, and
                     cumulative homeworks.

I) Grade Scale: 93 - 100 A   70 - 76 D
                     85 - 92 B   0 - 69 F
                     77 - 84 C

J) Extra Credit: Given often and is easily available
                     to everyone who SEES ME.

K) Symbols: BS - be specific
                     UN - Unacceptable
                      P - Paragraph Problems
                     SP - Mis-spelled word
                    INT - Interesting
                      N - Unclear; poorly said

L) Room Resources: $1.00 fine or assessed value if not
                     returned.

I have already explained my system for homework value points and the practice of lateness and penalty assessment. A further comment on this is necessary. Some teachers feel that the key lesson to be learned in assigning due dates is the responsibility of meeting deadlines. I partially agree and I certainly make students adhere to such deadlines on test and quiz makeups. But homework I view in a different light. I have always felt that it is better for the student to at least get the work done than to skip it altogether. Therefore I accept late homework at any time during a marking period, but the later it is, the greater the penalty assessment. I will drop the total all the way down to one-third of its on-time value if necessary. If you drop the grade points below one-third, the student will realize that it may not be even worthwhile to do the assignments.

As for tests and quizzes, I give them five school days to make up the work. Beyond that the retention factor minimizes and the backlog factor maximizes. If, after one school week the student fails to make up the test or quiz, I have been known to offer the test as a worksheet to be done on a take-home, open-note basis for extra or minimum credit, but this nowhere near approaches true test value. My thinking here is that tests are so large in weight that a zero truly hurts the final grade. In any case, however, the students must see me. This shows some initiative on their part.

Bear in mind that my system is for dealing with high school students. Certainly elementary school students should be taught the value of submitting work on time as a lesson in and of itself.

COMPETENCY TESTS are a different animal. The administration of competency tests is a practice that many schools have recently adopted to counter the high rates of student absenteeism. Accordingly, a student with a high number of days absent would be required to show his mastery or deficiencies in the subject area by taking such a test. The should be scored on a pass/fail basis. The concept has merit. However, the trick is to put the pressure on the student in this situation rather than taking it on yourself as just another demand on your time. You may wish to choose from either of these courses of action - a set time and place as in a structured examination where the student shows up and takes the test. Or you can give the test as a take-home, open-note worksheet that the student

must turn in. I choose the latter and on this test I
include a listing of missed assignments with a
requirement that the student submit this work; he must
submit his updated notebook as well. Furthermore, to
facilitate the ease of test administration, I simply
list standard essay questions and circle those that were
dealt with when the student was absent. Consider that
basically, what one should be looking for on a
competency test is whether or not the student has caught
up on his work and grasped the missed material. I feel
that it is ethically wrong for a teacher to view the
test as a tool of vengeance against a student who is
habitually absent. Let the front office deal with such
absentee recidivists through their policy structure; our
job is to teach. A typical competency test that I give
is included on the next page. One further note before
leaving this subject: in giving the general type of
competency test, as I do, it is quicker and easier to
photocopy a test page for a student and then circle the
appropriate questions than it is to make up a new and
different test for each competency you must administer.

RUSSIAN HISTORY: COMPETENCY TEST

MR. TRIMBLE   NAME_____

PASS:_____   FAIL:_____   DATE DUE:_____

____PART I: NOTEBOOK   Submit a satisfactory updated
                                 notebook including all class
                                 notes and handouts.

____PART II: ASSIGNMENTS   Submit all missed assignments,
                                 including homework, papers,
                                 quizzes, tests, etc.

____PART III:ESSAYS   Answer each of the essays
                                 circled below. These are to
                                 determine your ability to show
                                 competency in subject material
                                 covered during your absences.
                                 Answer only those circled.

1. Discuss the reforms of Catherine the Great.

2. Discuss the reforms of Tsar Alexander II.

3. How did the late Romonov tsar's contribute to the
   inevitability of the 1917 Russian Revolution? Be
   specific with regard to certain rulers.

4. Trace the trends toward revolution as exemplified by
   such groups as the Peoples' Will Party, the RSDLP,
   etc. Include the Revolution of 1905.

5. Discuss Karl Marx's theory of history and economics.

6. Discuss the Russian Revolution in terms of causes,
   events, people.

7. What did Lenin do to consolidate Bolshevik rule in
   Russia? Include the NEP and the Red-White Civil War.

8. How did Stalin rise to power and what did he do with
   his power?

9. Discuss Russian impact on World War II.

10. Argue that Russia is to blame for the Cold War.
    Conversely, argue that the U.S. is to blame.

The NOTEBOOK CHECK is another effective aspect of solid classroom management, especially with younger students encountering lecture methods for the first time, or with a class of poor academic proficiency. Write up a checklist of topics and handouts that the student should have. As they turn in their notebooks for grading, simply check off whether or not the material is included. Do this for a grade as it may motivate a non-note-taker to come up with a notebook. Furthermore, the checklist can show the student exactly what he or she may be missing. Include a check space for organization, too. Notes scattered on the back of a science ditto or on a lunchroom bag should be noted as inefficient. I have included a sample notebook check-sheet on the next page.

On several occasions I have mentioned handouts and dittos. What you hand out to students may range from drill sheets and homework assignments to political cartoons, cogent essays, or newspaper articles. If you find yourself handing out many of the same dittos semester after semester, an interesting approach is the RESOURCE BOOK. In effect you will be editing your own supplemental text by compiling all of the handouts, running off enough sets for one semester, binding them, and then lending them out to students to be returned later. Consider it. It saves the taxpayers' money, increases your efficiency, fosters student organization, and makes you look good in the classroom and before the Board of Education. Do not hesitate to add an essay or two by yourself, either. It is a tremendous ego-feed to pass out "your book" at the beginning of the semester. The students respect it. Realize, however, that you will probably be adding, editing, and re-arranging every few years. No author is ever satisfied with his or her work. In some classes of very current subject material, a resource booklet like this can be better than a formal text which becomes outdated so easily.

Advanced academic classes, in which you require primary source readings, can be enhanced by the edition of a RESOURCE BOOK. Simply run off the short readings that you most often use each year and bind them up for distribution to the students. I have found, since I am continually reading at least one book which is a primary source, that my files continue to grow, so the book needs to be updated every few years. On that vein, after finishing any primary source book, go back and photocopy key areas which you probably underlined or highlighted. This is how your eventual Resource Book will be compiled.

WORLD HISTORY   NAME:

MR. TRIMBLE   DATE:

         NOTEBOOK CHECK: MARKING PERIOD I

_____STUDENT RULES & REGULATIONS   _____FALL OF ROME

_____COURSE OUTLINE   _____MIDDLE AGES

_____ANCIENT NEAR EAST & EGYPT   _____STRUCTURE OF
                                        MEDIEVAL CHURCH

_____ANCIENT GREECE   _____RENAISSANCE

_____GOLDEN AGE   _____REFORMATION

_____ANCIENT ROME   _____ORGANIZATION

GRADE:

COMMENTS:

Another very important aspect of efficient classroom management lies in the area of TESTING. Let us first consider the design and structure of tests. Philosophically, I feel that tests should be major grades and that they should be given less frequently than quizzes and homework. They should therefore hold significant weight. This should be even further emphasized if you teach college-bound juniors and seniors as they will, in most cases, encounter such conditions in college - few tests, but of considerable weight. There is of course, the counter-argument that the more tests, then the more grades for averaging and thus a more accurate assessment of the students' work. Both schemes hold merit so it is advisable to consider the grade level (more tests should be given to junior high school-aged students, including freshmen), subject area (drill classes such as math and foreign languages would benefit from more tests, perhaps even weekly), and academic level of the students (the poorer the student, the more tests as in order to cut down on the volume of material to be tested on and perhaps help him attain a higher grade.)

When considering the actual structure of tests, I have always been a believer in essays. The trend of late has somewhat gravitated away from the essay and I feel this is misguided. What with Scholastic Aptitude Tests being multiple choice and the availability of modern test scoring machines, it is small wonder that many of us just plop down on the kids' desks a five-page multiple choice exam that we have been using for three years.

There are problems with this trend. As Banesh Hoffman showed decades ago, in The Tyranny of Testing, multiple-choice tests do not allow interpretative answers to be correct. As Jacques Barzun suggested in a 1988 op-ed essay in the N.Y. Times, ("Multiple Choice Flunks Out," 10/12/88) multiple-choice tests fragment information and do not allow students to develop writing skills, envision flow and continuity in the subject material, or consider relationships in the bits of information that they are attempting to learn. Moreover, I suggest that multiple choice tests penalize those students who know more about the test subject. With reflection, they can often make a case for any of several answers offered, yet only one is scored as "correct."

A good essay examination takes imagination. It should combine large blocks of notes into single questions. For example, rather than inquire what the Glorious Revolution was in English History, ask the student to trace the parliamentary-crown struggles from 1628 to 1688. Critics may suggest that this is too broad a topic, but I feel that high school students should see progressions and developmental factors rather than just lonely, isolated facts. Another suggestion is to give the students a choice of essays, perhaps allowing him to select two out of three to answer. No one can be equally adept at all phases of the material presented in class (even we teachers have our strong and weak areas). And be sure to allow for, even demand, analysis on the part of the student. This is education - making the student analyze and deduce. Essays force a child to do this. Furthermore, essays better prepare the student for what he or she will face upon leaving school. Colleges demand papers and essays; the work force does not give you multiple-choice bulletins to write. Our lives call for us to write letters and memos, not true-false questions.

Of course, be fair to all students in the classroom, as some may be more adept at essay-writing than others. Most of my tests are 30-50 percent essay; the remaining portion will be terms, fill-ins, true-false, matching, etc. I will vary this according to grade level and intellectual level; however, students of lower academic skills may receive fewer essays, or at least essays that are more structured and direct. Freshman would receive essays of a more objective nature, calling for more factual recall than analysis. The writing of good essays must be taught, and this will be dealt with later in the book.

I have included two sample tests. The World History test is designed for freshmen while the Russian History test is more for upper-level students.

WORLD HISTORY   NAME:_____
MR. TRIMBLE   DATE:_____
TEST III: 1600 - 1815

PART I: ESSAYS   Choose any five of the seven given.
                  Each is worth 10 points. <u>Be specific</u>!

  1. Discuss the causes of the French Revolution
  2. Peter the Great was an absolute monarch - what
     was that, who was he, and what did he do?

3. Louis XIV (14) was an absolute monarch - what was that, who was he, and what did he do?
4. Discuss the Enlightenment, the philosophies, their areas of attack, and the enlightened despots.
5. Trace events in the English Civil War - discuss cause and effect.
6. Discuss the importance of and accomplishments of Napoleon Bonaparte.
7. Why was the Congress of Vienna important?

PART II: NAMES AND MATCHING Each is worth two points.

___Robespierre
___Napoleon

___Charles I

___Louis XIV (14)

___Louis XVI (16)

___Oliver Cromwell

___Peter I the Great

___Frederick II the Great

___Ivan III the Great

___Ivan IV the Terrible

___Catherine II the Great

A) rise of Prussia
B) conquered most of Europe, but lost in Russia and at Waterloo
C) Headed Comm. of Public Safety during French Revolution - king
D) beheaded during English Civil War - king
E) beheaded during French Revolution - king
F) Tsar of Russia in 1700
G) Puritan general who briefly took power during English Civil War
H) built Versailles palace and broke power of the nobles in France
I) expelled Mongols from Russia - 1500
J) eradicated nobility class in Russia with mass executions
K) none of these

PART III: EVENTS AND MATCHING Each is worth two points.

___Congress of Vienna

___Age of Absolutism

A) height of French Revolution: 20,000 lost their heads
B) French Revolution - 5-man rule government

____Enlightenment

____Enlightenment despots

____Estates General

____House of Commons

____Philosophes

____Roundheads/Cavaliers

____Code Napoleon

____Reign of Terror

____Consul government

____Directory government

____Flight to Varennes

____guillotine

C) French Revolution - 3-man rule government
D) French fortress/prison stormed in July, 1789
E) political parties in English Civil War: parliament and crown
F) Kings had total power
G) writers during Enlightenment
H) French Revolution - took king's power away; he fled
I) settled map of Europe after Napoleon; summit conference; balance of power; peace
J) invaders into Russia; historically retarded their growth
K) kings and queens who followed ideas of the Enlightenment
L) most powerful division of English parliament
M) another name of Enlightenment
N) law code for France
O) Napoleon last battle
P) when Louis XVI fled France with intent of returning and over-throwing revolu-tionary govern-ment; caught

___Bastille	Q) machine used to remove ones' head from his body
___Waterloo	R) English king has never been power-ful after this event; James II overthrown and Commons rules ever since
___Constitution of 1791	S) French parliament consisting of three houses in 1789
___Glorious Revolution 1791	T) epoch in European History when writers attacked absolute kingship, believing that people should have say in government
___Age of Reason	
___Mongols	U) none of these

(It should be noted that each "part" of a test should be confined to single or easily accessible pages.)

NAME:_____
DATE:_____

PART I: ESSAYS   Choose any two of the three given -
                    only two. Each is worth 25 points, so
                    be complete and fully detailed.

          1. Compare and contrast the foreign policies of
             Peter I and Catherine II. Evaluate.
          2. Trace the course of events in the Time of
             Troubles.
          3. Fully discuss the domestic reforms of Peter
             the Great. Evaluate.

PART II: TERMS   Each is worth 5 points. Define and
                    discuss the importance of each.
                    Choose 8 of 10.

          1. Ulozhenie of 1649:

          2. Roskolnik:

          3. Partitions of Poland:

          4. Nakaz:

          5. enlightened despotism:

          6. Northern War:

          7. Age of Favorites:

          8. Pugachev Uprising:

          9. "Boyar Tsar":

          10. False Dmitry:

PART III: MATCHING   For 2 points each, match names
                       with deeds.

          ____Prince Potemkin   A) patriarch of Muscovy
                                      who played
                                      significant role in
          ____Catherine II   Time of Troubles
                                   B) king of Sweden; lost
                                      to Peter the Great in
          ____Peter I   Northern War

	C)	consort of Catherine II; successful war vs. Turks
___Alexis		
	D)	first Romanov ruler
___Michael I	E)	replaced Fedor II; his ineptitude began the Time of troubles
___Filaret & Hermogen		
	F)	birth of modern Russia; Baltic seacoast; Holy Synod
___Boris Gudonov		
___Elizabeth		
	G)	daughter of Peter I; favorite; Winter Palace; wins Finland
___Charles XII		
	H)	increased serfdom; Nikon caused problems for him
	I)	non-Romonov who improved Russian status in Western Europe; southern outlet to the sea
	J)	none of these

TEST SECURITY

Cheating is inevitable, but the teacher must make an effort to minimize it. Obviously, cheating invalidates a test and the test results, so one must be cognizant of not only cheating techniques, but also security measures. This portion of my book deals with the security aspect. A discussion of cheating techniques could probably fill volumes and would certainly be counter-productive here.

A) Separation of desks - the oldest and most often used method, but be sure to remove the suspected cheater from his home turf and/or away from the desk where he has scribbled his crib notes or arranged his "onlook" system with a partner in crime.

B) Separation of cliques - divide and conquer is the applicable adage here. Remove the cheater from his compatriots.

C) Paper - provide all paper, thus preventing essays and problems written out at home from being submitted on test day. This is especially true in cases where you inform the students, in the class review, of essays that might appear on the exam. Also, providing paper eliminates the quick glance at a notebook page as the student reaches for paper from his own source.

D) "Everything off your desks and out of your desks" - For those of you who teach in classrooms with old-style desks containing book storage compartments under the desk top, be aware that this is a good space for cheaters to write notes or hide cheat-sheets. Have them place their books and other materials on the floor at their feet, face down. One lucky day - true story here - I caught nine kids with cheat sheets in their desks during a freshman World History class.

E) Be mobile - Nothing unsettles the cheater more than the teacher who is not in a set pattern. Float around the room, often standing in back of the room to observe.

F) If the student is looking at you, suspect that he is cheating - The student who sleeps during your lecture but is suddenly enraptured by your countenance during exam times is often trying to get away with something. Keep an eye on him.

G) Penalty points- Many of us are intimidated by our own system. By this I mean that we know a zero on a key test may seal the fate of a student, so we are reluctant to penalize them with a zero for a ripped up, cheated-upon test. One way to get around this is to impose a penalty of five or ten points off when you catch him or her cheating. Usually the student is so relieved to have been caught but not fully prosecuted with the Big Zero that he does not further challenge you. The penalty assessment of 5 - 10 points usually negates the points gained illegally, too. The message is sent and the entire class receives it. Of course, the hard-core cheater must be dealt with to the maximum.

H) Send home the cheated-on test - Emblazon the test with "0 - Cheating" in bright red ink and send it home. This prevents a recurrence and it does meet out a little justice. It is most certainly a good form of reality-therapy for parents.

I) Think ahead - Be suspicious. The student who asks to wear his stereo headphones, telling you that music makes him think just may have a tape full of answers. Check watches to see that they do not have calculators, math teachers. Be sure that all notes have been well-erased from the blackboards and that all

relevant charts and maps have been removed from the
bulletin board. Be observant - I have seen notes
written inside arm slings, on palms, on legs as students
sit crossed-legged, inside jackets, and even on tiny
edible scrolls written on grocery register tape.
Cheaters are ingenious - if they only spent as much time
studying as they do devising new ways to cheat....

J) Make different copies of test - A lot different
approaches can be used here, but first and foremost is
to minimize the repetition of tested material from class
to class on your tests. Students at the beginning of
the day have a well established network of communication
with the students at the end of the day and most
certainly your test data will be widely known. Along
another vein, I have always thought it questionable to
use the same tests year after year. Copies will get
around. Even if you collect your test copies and do not
return them, to give the same test year after year
reflects a certain degree of rigidity in your teaching.
I find that, at most, I can get three years out of a
test before I find it outdated either due to new
material I have emphasized or questions I have
re-phrased. Of course, there will be standardized or
departmental tests that are used to measure baseline
comparisons, but even these should be revised regularly
and most certainly they should deal with objective
content rather than interpretation. For example, to ask
if Japan fought on the side of America in World War II
is certainly objective, and every History teacher would
be hard- pressed to defend an affirmative answer here.
But to ask for the basic cause of the Thirty Years War
would be a subjective question that probably varies from
teacher to teacher and should therefore be eliminated,
or re-phrased. Such a question could read: "Which of
the following was NOT a cause for the Thirty Year War?"
Some teachers like to occasionally give an open-book or
open-note test. Although I have never been a big fan of
these, they can serve to reward good note-takers in
class and help the students get by on a test that you
know is difficult. One thought however, is to not tell
the students in advance that you plan to give them their
test in open-book fashion. They simply will not study.
Students fail to realize that open-book tests, if not
prepared for in advance, can be more difficult than
conventional tests as the students spend the bulk of the
test time looking up answers.

What about a "legal cheat sheet (LCS). Pass out
a 3 x 5 card and allow students to write down what they
feel is the most important data in the unit to be
tested. Tell them they will be allowed to have this
card, and only this card, in front of them during the

46

test. This works. Students will inadvertantly study by trying discern what is important enough to be written on the LCS. This idea came from a 1989 student teacher, Mr. Edward Peters from Monmouth College. I used it in a low-academic class which had just completed a long, complex unit of material.

Returning to the concept of differing test topics, the procedure can be fairly simple. After making up one test, you can cut and paste questions in a different order and then photocopy or otherwise reproduce it. Two different tests are usually sufficient, three copies at most. Differing copies can be color coded with a felt-tip pen and distributed to different rows or to alternate seats. If you teach the same subject to several different classes, then you may wish to leave about thirty per cent of the test questions blank and write different questions on the blackboard. Makeup tests can be handled in a similar fashion. Even if you have not made up differing copies of the same test, just tell the students that you have and pass them out in a concerned, varied fashion, bluffing all the way. Tell them to, "be sure to write the test number on the answer sheet because the tests are different."

To be frank, most teachers do not go through all this. However, I do not feel that it costs all that much extra time; just be organized. Secondly, the kids seem to respect this type of thinking as "street-wise."

One final thought - do not make a big thing of test security in an outward sense. To be a militant gendarme, hawking in on everybody and accusing all is to lower yourself. Merely accept the fact that cheating can occur, that you can take professional measures to minimize it, and then do so without argument or discussion, wearing a smile as you do it. Tell the kids that you are "removing temptation." They will accept it much better than the pedantic, charlatan approach.

Take it as some comfort that a 1985 survey of 5000 junior high school students showed that 78 per cent never cheat, 14 per cent rarely cheat, 7 per cent sometimes cheat and less than 1 per cent often cheat.

An item of classroom organization that can help your students is what I call the STUDENT STUDY GUIDE. As can be seen, I have taken the liberty to include a copy of the one that I pass out to each and every student on the first day of school. I do not insist that they use it or even read it, but I have much positive feedback from those who do.

Although not its intent, the Study Guide can help those teachers who might be held accountable for teaching study skills to students. Basically, the ideas contained in it are those that I use or have stumbled upon in my ongoing study as I continue to take college courses. In preparing one for your students, cut and paste, add and delete, and tie in peculiarities that you might employ in your own study methods.

STUDENT STUDY GUIDES

"All you've ever wanted to know about note-taking, test study, oral reports, outlining, term paper research, etc., but were afraid to ask...."

R. M. Trimble
Manasquan High School
November, 1984

NOTE TAKING

1. Have a separate notebook or section of notebook for each course. Scattering notes on separate pieces of paper only leads to scattered thoughts, no continuity, and a lack of organization.

2. Never write in full sentences; rarely write verbatim notes.

3. Listen as you write.

4. If a teacher writes it on the board, you should write it in your notebook.

5. Devise your own set of symbols to simplify and speed up notetaking.   EXAMPLES: w/   - with

inc.	- including	sig.	- significance
. .	- therefore	est.	- establish
-->	- leads to	c.	- approximately
>	- greater than	i.e.	- explain something
<	- less than	*	- important to note
ch.	- chapter	+	- and
p.	- page	$	- cost or money
ex.	- example	#	- number

   You can set your own symbols, but remember - abbreviate whenever possible.   (**)
      (ab.)   (poss.)

6. Organize your notes on a page by numbering and indenting when necessary.   EXAMPLE: Causes of WWI
   1. Hunger - power status, colonies, markets
                  Ind. Rev. and Age of Imperialism
                  *power vacuums (areas of sig. that no
                  power controls)
   2. Fear --> alliances
                  Central Powers: Germ., Turkey, Austria,
                  Hungary Allies: U.S., Eng., France,
                  Italy, Russia
      and so on....

7. If you are out of class, copy by hand or photocopy notes from a reliable classmate. If you will be out of an extended period of time, have a student either tape record class or copy with a piece of carbon paper you provide.

8. Keep all handouts and dittos in your notebook. Paste them in so they will not get lost.

TESTS

1. Knowing you have a test in advance, try the note-reading method.
   a. Two days before test, simply read through your notes (15 minutes).

   b. Read through them again at another sitting.

   c. Third reading - the night before, perhaps - read through and jot down on separate piece of paper the key points to know.

   d. Carrying this piece of paper around, glance at it during brief interludes of inactivity (i.e. - the lunchroom, in-between classes, on the phone with a boring person)

   e. This should set you, but if possible, re-read the notes, emphasizing in your mind the key concepts.

2. Essays:
   a. Construct, in your mind, what the essays will be if the teacher has not given them beforehand; you can usually identify them as broad blocks of related notes, cause and effect, analysis, contrast and compare, etc.

   b. Once identified, draw up a skeleton outline of what should be in the essays and put that to memory (some teachers may allow you to have them check your over outline before the test).

   c. When taking the test, simply fill meat and muscle into the skeleton (outline).

3. True - false tests can usually be handled by the note-reading method alone.

4. Fill-in tests can best be studied by jotting down basic terms and studying them.

5. Multiple choice tests, once taken, must be looked over for checking before submitting to teachers; if teachers give trick questions, they are contained, usually, in this type of question. If an answer reads, "Only A & D" or "all of the above," check these out-they oftentimes are the real answer. Do not jump on the first right answer in a series.

6. Be sure to pay close attention to numbers when they are given in answers. Teachers often slip in trick, similar-sounding numbers to fool you.

ASSIGNMENTS

1. Write them down, don't try to remember them.

2. Either buy a little pocket notebook or take a piece of paper and fold it into 1/4's so that you can literally list assignments for over a week by flipping the sides (keep it in your pocket or wallet).

3. If you have a reading assignment due somewhat ahead, divide the number of pages up by the number of nights you have to read it; this alleviates cramming on the night before it is due; book reports should be handled in the same manner - read ten pages per night, or so on.

4. NEVER copy directly from a textbook when assigned chapter questions - teachers will grade down on this; also re-read your own answers to make sure that they make sense.

BOOK REVIEWS AND OUTLINES

1. When outlining a chapter consider this:
   if you own the book, you can underline in the book what should be remembered; of course, in most cases you do NOT own the book, so jot down what you normally would have underlined. Keep outlines brief - write only what is to be remembered.

2. In writing book reports; what are the author's main points? What made him write this book aside from a desire for fame and money? He has a message - what is it?

3. Do not write in full, flowery sentences; write in clear note-form.

4. For the purpose of a book review, jot down notes about the author's writing style; outline the book for content and be critical in your analysis.

5. Do NOT review a book by saying "Chapter 1 says this and Chapter 2 says that."

6. NEVER begin ANY essay or book review with the word, "Well,.."

7. Don't bother with pictures.

8. Most teachers ask for a cover page containing title, author, publisher, and your name, class, date.

9. Read carefully - a teacher of mine once said that if you know what's next without turning the page, you are reading carefully.

10. In my book reviews, I ask for a summary in which you basically outline the book (and prove to me that you read it), a critical analysis in which you note what is specifically good or bad about the book, and a word on the value of the book (i.e. - whether it will help you in the understanding of the course you are writing it for).

ORAL REPORTS

1. Don't clutch...practice your oral report at home.

2. Tie in any audio-visual aids you can (photos, maps, dittos, charts).

3. NEVER read your report...in fact, do not even write in full sentences on your note cards.

4. On your note cards, number them and write large so that you can easily refer to them and keep track.

5. Speak to the audience, not to the paper.

6. Don't be afraid to smile, walk about, and point to audio-visual aids.

TERM PAPER

1. Many teachers advocate the 3 x 5 card system for research and this is fine, but many alternatives exist and I offer this one:
    a) Obtain a separate notebook for research purposes.
    b) On the top of the page, write down all data that you will need for the bibliography and then proceed to take your notes like this:
        p. 47 - author shows bias toward Kennedy
        p. 56 - Cuban Missile Crisis called for mobilization of 23 naval vessels
        p. 101 - see photocopy one
        p. 115 - Kennedy wanted LBJ to refuse VP role
    c) Jot down your notes on one side of each page; leave the back blank.
    d) Attach any photocopied pages by staple to the back of each notebook page; note that these pages may contain copious passages that demand a full reprinting in your paper.
    e) As you use a particular passage, cross it out of your research book.
    f) Repeat the process with each book you use for research
        -- this system allows you to keep everything together, rather than flipping through cards, plus it allows for photocopies to be more easily handled.
        -- when constructing footnotes, plug in your noted pages with the appropriate numbers in your footnote sequence.
    g) When through with the rough draft of paper, go through the research book to see if you missed anything.
2. What should be footnoted?
    Statistics
    Quotations (verbatim passages in the author's words)
    Unusual Author Notations (things that the author, and no one else, says - give him credit for the concept, not you). Yes, it spells out SQUAN* (sorry about that)

---

*I teach at Manasquan High School -- nickname Squan

3. Don't cite encyclopedias on bibliographies - this is a tacky move; use them for background ideas, but there is no need to cite them and NEVER copy from them.

4. Pictures aren't necessary, but at times maps are.

5. Know that teachers can easily spot plagiarism by the change in writing styles - AVOID IT.

6. Have someone else proof-read your paper before it is written in final draft - they can spot your misspellings easier than you can.

7. Be sure to utilize the index and table of contents in a book before determining its value to your research. Do not pull book after book off the shelf just because they vaguely touch upon your topic. Check out what pages and chapters you might need and then read only them. You need not read every word of every book.

8. Just for your reference, I have included a copy of the Dewey Decimal System used by every major library. If you are not already familiar with it, then this will help.

THE SUBJECT DIVISIONS ARE:

000-099 General Works (encyclopedias)	500-599 Science
100-199 Philosophy	600-699 Useful Arts
200-299 Religion	700-799 Fine Arts
300-399 Social Science	800-899 Literature
400-499 Language	900-999 History

THE STUDY ATMOSPHERE

I know... you can study and do homework with the stereo, T.V., and radio on... YOU ARE KIDDING YOURSELF. Sure, you can tune out the music for brief moments, but when it comes to concentrated study effort, this cannot be done for long periods of time. It's that simple. Turn off the sound and sights. Two things will happen: you will get your homework done faster and you will get it done better.

PART IV

TEACHING

"...A teacher must have the energy of a harnessed
  volcano, the efficiency of an adding machine,
  the memory of an elephant, the understanding of
  a psychiatrist, the wisdom of Solomon, the
  tenacity of a spider...the decisiveness of a
  general, the diplomacy of an ambassador...
  From my regular visits to schools, I know there's
  little exaggeration in that description. We
  expect an awful lot from teachers. And too
  often their heroic toil goes unrecognized."

                                    Richard Celeste
                                    Ohio Governor

"It is liberal learning which, after all, prepares
  students for the changes that their lives and
          careers will ask of them."

                                    James Lackenmier

EFFECTIVE LECTURING

It has been said that speech is taught, but speaking is a gift. I agree, but there are some hints that can help enhance each teacher's ability to speak.

a) <u>Animation</u> - Did you ever wonder why it is sometimes difficult to stay awake in a church sermon? The answer is easy - the pulpit is the problem. As nice as a lectern might look in a classroom, avoid it like the plague. Move about, gesticulate, animate -- keep your kids awake. Utilize the entire room; do not restrict yourself to a frontal corridor. Ease into the middle of the room when talking, sit off-handedly at an empty desk, scramble to the wall charts and then back to the blackboard. Drift on over to where a student is sleeping. Some critics may call this theatrics, but the bottom line is that it works. The students are forced to follow your pattern about the room.

b) <u>The Contact Pattern</u> - Each classroom has a certain pattern of eye contact -- students that you find yourself teaching to. This is natural and most often stimulated by the oral or visual response you elicit from a particular student. The patterns traditionally fall into geometric shapes such as these.

You will find that each class will fall into its own pattern. The trick is to expand the contact zone (shaded) to make certain that you teach to as many students as possible. Hit the dead zones by purposely calling on students in those areas or by walking into these areas as you gyrate around the room. Some teachers will assign seats with this pattern in mind, mixing in motivated students with disaffected ones. I find, however, that this can stifle spontaneity and responses, so I prefer to let kids sit where they may and I do the work of waking up the dead zones. Also, while delivering your material use actual names of students to show examples. Let us say that you want to show how feudalism developed. Point to Johnny and call him a peasant; say that Jean is a lord and that Billy is a knight. This wakes up sleepers and can force you to hit the "dead zones" in your room.

c) <u>Voice Inflection</u> - Listen to a good evangelist speaker and take note of how he leads his listeners by lowering his voice and then blasts them with a key point made in an octave or two higher. This is a simple, yet effective device -- raise and lower your voice as necessary. Stop-phrases that grab the students' attention, such as "Here's the key...," "Two reasons why...," "Now, make note of this...," "In conclusion...," or "Listen up...," followed by a short pregnant pause are definite aids to effective lecturing.

d) <u>Audio-Visual Aids</u> - Films and filmstrips have their purpose, but it is not in place of the teacher. Use audio-visual aids as a supplement, not as a replacement for lecturing. Students can benefit from a good, curriculum-related and properly introduced film or filmstrip. Generally it is good to teach along with it by stopping to emphasize points or to clarify. Instead of an entire video or film, why not show a short, pre-recorded clip? Just ten minutes of the guillotine scene from " A Tale Of Two Cities" shows the Reign of Terror more vividly than you can ever describe. There is no need to show the entire movie to punctuate your lecture. Records and tapes are generally not effective with high school students. They simply do not keep the kids' attention. I have used them as background supplement when students are working quietly at their desks, however. Perhaps this is a sign of the times -- television in lieu of radio. Employ show-n-tell sequences of artifacts, maps, photos, etc.

The use of the overhead projector is a very solid lecture-enhancement device. Your essential concepts can be accentuated, time is saved from laboriously writing all of the notes on the blackboard, and with the over-head you can ensure a proper lecture flow from class to class. By this I mean that if you have several classes of the same content, over-head transparencies will ensure that you do not show or forget to cover certain items. In addition, the over-head can be used to show duplicated material that you have passed around to the students.

For example, graphs, charts, and maps can be photocopied, distributed to the students and then referred to with an identical copy flashed on the screen. Furthermore, maps can be shown on the black-board and then drawn on with chalk to depict battle strategies and changing borders.

I have also used the over-head projector for lessons on political cartoons, correcting essays and grammar before the entire class, short readings for class interpretation, and instructional lessons in my coaching fields, for instance in baseball by projecting a diamond on the blackboard and drawing plays and strategies. When using the blackboard, I tell the students that what I write up there should go in their notebooks. Also, pick up some colored chalk as it accentuates a blackboard presentation nicely.

e) <u>Handouts</u> - Duplicated material can be another important aid to your lectures. Handouts can be used in the manner referred to above for the over-head projector -- as a punctuation and accentuation device. Handouts can be used in another way, however. If you are teaching a class of students with lower academic capabilities, give them copies of notesheets on which they fill in your lecture points. This gives them the feel of what should be noted and what should merely be listened to. Hint - there is a tendency to dictate verbatim when using this method, so realize it and avoid it. When a student asks you to repeat a definition, throw the question back out to the class. Also, if you have a large block of material to cover and not enough time to do it, hand out notesheets. This will expedite things surprisingly. The problem with handout notesheets is that they will often be scattered about the notebook, if kept at all. You must monitor this by periodically checking student notebooks. The basic message here is that you must try to incorporate as much variety into your presentation as possible.

f) <u>Question-Answer</u> - An interesting study was done on teacher-student response time allowed for questions. The general time lapse between a teacher posing a question and then answering it himself when no student volunteered was less than four seconds. The purpose of the study was to show that increased allowance for time after a question is posed will draw more answers. It may seem obvious, but it is true that teachers do not like long lapses of silence following their questions. Students are often reluctant to respond even when they know the correct answer. Another hint is that when you get one of those long pauses of non-answers, specifically ask a student. Perhaps he can offer something to build on. By allowing more time after a question, you can draw more answers or at least partial answers on which you can build a deductive reasoning process toward the response you want. Furthermore, as a student responds to a question, move away from him or

her. This forces the answerer to raise her/his voice
and thus makes her/him more audible to the entire class.

You as a teacher must force yourself to ask
questions of the class. All too often, we get into our
lectures and forget that the kids might not be following
us. Make a point, stop and ask a relevant question.
Benjamin S. Bloom's famous taxonomy (Longman's, 1956)
suggests the following organizational concepts to the
issue of question-answer techniques:

1) There are knowledge questions in which the
teacher approaches material from a trivia-like position.
For example, "With what president do we associate the
New Deal?"

2) There are comprehensive questions -- ask your
students to explain cause and effect, why and
results. An example here might be, "What were the
causes of the American Civil War?"

3) Application Questions -- These call for the
student to use what they have learned. For example,
"Knowing what you do about ecosystems and checks and
balances in nature, what did Adlai Stevenson mean by
his famous `Spaceship Earth` analogy? Give me some
explicit examples."

4) Analysis questions call for the student to
identify motives, to deduce conclusions, etc. "In the
study of history, is it the man who makes the events or
is it the events and the time that make the man?"

5) Synthesis questions include hypothetical
questions that call for new ideas; problem-solving
questions would be included in this category. An
example would be, "What was the real motivation behind
the Founding Fathers' creation of the Electoral
College in the Constitution?"

6) Evaluation Questions -- Simply stated, these
ask for opinions based on fact. An example here would
be, "Who do you think is the best king England ever
had?"*

The results of a surprising, and disturbing, study
once showed that only seven minutes out of each 150
classroom minutes were devoted to question-answer. This
must be increased by all of us.

*from Motivation & Teaching: A Practical Guide, by
Raymond J. Wledhewski, NEA Publishing

When it comes to questions from students, unless the answer calls for a sharp, pithy response, try to re-direct as many questions as possible. Answer like, "Well, what do you think?" or "Can someone else help him with that one?" Another point is to try to accept as many responses from the class to each question as you can. This invites a more open and free-flowing line of dialogue in the classroom. Allow as many hands to answer each question as possible and then build on each one for the answer you want. Each child will feel that he contributed.

Since questioning is so crucial to a good lesson, it is not unwise to write certain essential questions out in advance and write them into your lesson plans. Call on the daydreaming student as often as possible as this helps build overall attentiveness in class. Also, use as much positive reinforcement as possible in listening to student responses. There is usually something in what a student says that you can build on, some kernel of truth that you can cite, or some direction that you can take with his answer. Try to avoid the abrupt, demeaning "No!"

Remember to avoid verbosity in phrasing your questions. The longer the text of the question, the less the students stay with you. Try to avoid phrasing two questions into one. Make sure that students have answered your question before you go on to the next one. When a student has his hand raised, be sure that you stop to answer his inquiry before phrasing your own. And lastly, try to avoid the yes/no question that does little to stimulate any discussion.

g) <u>Miscellaneous</u> - Other facets that come to mind include the use of puns and quips. High school kids can be severe critics when it comes to teachers' jokes. Most of your carefully prepared "material" will fall flat. However, they love puns. Quickly slipped in, they can liven up a lecture and snap the daydreamers back to the classroom. Do not worry about the quality of the puns -- the worse, the better sometimes. To be sure, there will be groans, but allow your ego to handle it.

Avoid reading long passages. Certainly a truism for any lecture, but sometimes a particularly well-written passage, usually of vivid gore and blood-lust, can enhance a lecture. Look for readings that help bring a particular portion of your material to life. In history, look for battle scenes or biographical passages; in English, perhaps a portion of classic prose.

Develop your lecture into a specific theme or message. Harvard Sinologist John King Fairbank once said that an effective lecture enables a listener to "hear a mind think." Therefore it behooves the lecturer to synthesize the material to be presented. Do not spin out a textbook's verbatim thoughts; do not stride page for page through the book. Take the book's idea as well your own interpretations. Take material that you have learned in your autodidactic study as well as in your college and graduate courses and blend it, refine it, translate it. Consider this: as you develop your lectures, are you hitting upon new ideas of causality, effect, and discovery as you present your material? If the answer is consistently no, then you have become stale. Overcome this by picking up a book or two on the subject; attend a seminar. Read more - infuse more data into your mental computer. Or perhaps try an audio-visual approach. Year after year, your presentations on the same subject should never sound and look the same. Begin each day's lecture with a short review of the previous day's material. If you teach a course with developmental sequences such as in history, or science, or English, do not start where you left off yesterday. Begin with a short, snappy question-answer period to set and background and build up to today's material. Let the students keep their notebooks open otherwise this review time will drag. More confidence is given this way, also. This method takes little or no extra time and is very effective for starting off a lecture. Also, It is sound educational practice to wrap up the day's lesson with a similarly brief review of key points to be remembered.

As far as the lecture notes that you employ are concerned, several methods can be considered. I have already mentioned the use of the over-head projector. What is flashed on the screen can serve as your lecture notes just as easily as they can be taken as class notes by your students. Similarly, handouts can serve as your lecture notes. I have seen teachers use spiral binders in which they have outlined lecture after lecture with spaces provided for additions and notations. Lecture notes can be written on 5 x 7" index cards, although these can be cumbersome. Single sheets containing notes that you wish to cover are the most common, but follow a couple of guidelines in preparing them. For one, never write in full sentences as there will be temptation to read to the class. Secondly, write with enough spacing so as to not lose your place. Thirdly, highlight and/or capitalize key items for easy reference. Fourthly, add on readings that you will wish to tie in, audio-visual aids, and even relevant homework

assignments. I have included my lecture notes on some
standard presentations I give in certain social studies
classes.

A highly significant study by Sacony indicated that
students remember 10 percent of what they read, 20
percent of what they hear, 30 percent of what they see,
50 percent of what they see and hear, 70 percent of what
they see and talk about, and 90 percent of what they
talk about as they perform. It has also been postulated
that a student will forget within three months fully 85
percent of what is learned by memorization!

RICHARD TRIMBLE   PLAN/DATE:

CLASS: ECOLOGY   GRADE LEVEL: 11 - 12

LESSON: (Instructional Objective): AIR POLLUTION

HOMEWORK ASSIGNMENT:

CONTENT: Notes, Concepts, Etc.

```
        a. intro - ditto; cost ext. 11 bill. $ yr.,
                nation death and cancers
        b. types of a.p.  1. natural
                          2. particulate - soft coal;
                             asbestos; LA-400 tons/day
                          3. chemical - unseen
                                carcinogenic
                                chemical changes &
                                   mixtures
        SO, No, CO, hydrocarbons       synthetic
        lead, C02, pesticides, etc.  corrosive &
                                        debilitative

cite article on back.........70% of all a.p. is chemical
                          4. smog - smoke & fog
                             photochemical car exhaust
                             (LA & London)
        c. sources of a.p. - industry 20%
                             cars   60%
                             space heating 10%
                             incineration & misc.   10%

        d. specific a.p. problems -
           1. Hothouse effect - fossil fuel combustion
                       (20% more CO2 by 2000 yr.)
           2. Temperature inversion - Denora, Pa.;
                                           London
           3. Ozone destruction - include SST
           4. Acid Rain
           5. Global Gloom - Chicago sunlight reduced
                       by 40%
           6. Climatic alterations
           7. Illnesses - heart attack, lung cancer
                       (55,000 die each year),
                       chronic bronchitis,
                       emphysema, bronchial asthma,
                       colds, pneumonia
           8. CO2 - Fossil fuels and de-forestation
```

```
        e. solutions - Clean Air Act of 1970 deadlines
                       and emissions controls
                       scrubbers, electrostatic
                       percipators, catalytic
                       converters alts. to fossil fuels
                       mass transit in urbans
                       Ringlemen Smoke Chart
                       greenbelts can reduce
                        particulates by 50%
                       burn-off
Miscellaneous Notes/Comments: rust occurs 30 x faster in
                       urban areas
                       steel corrodes 2 - 4 x
                                          faster
                       agric. loss 100/mill/$/yr.
                       electrostatic precips. can
                       remove 99% flyash
```

U.S. HISTORY II

LESSON PLAN: <u>U.S. IN W.W.I</u>

RICHARD M. TRIMBLE

1. entry - ditto
2. impact - tip scales
3. battles - St. Mihiel, Belleau Wood, Chateau-Thierry
           --Meuse-Argonne offensive
           --Pershing and unity
4. armistice and Treaty of Versailles
5. Wilson 's 14 Points - use map
6. Versailles Conf. - Big Four & contributions
                       Clemenceau - war guilt
                                    reparations/indemnity
                                    occupation
                                    seizure of industries
                       Wilson's predictions
7. Senate - isolationism
           Irreconcilables - Borah, Smith, Lodge
           tour & stroke
8. judgment of history on this era
9. Intervention Episode

64

R. TRIMBLE

ANTHROPOLOGY

LESSON 13

"CULTURE"

1. definition

2. how influences us - examples

3. discuss: norms

        mores

        sanctions

        culture shock

        ethnocentricity

        primitivity

        acculturation - assimilation
                                 absorption

        subcultures (overhead)

        culture lag

4. blue laws - read examples

5. assign - cultural change interview

        subcultures chart

One way to enhance your lectures is with the use of pictures and hands-on material. To wait for a film-strip often puts your comments out of context and subjects them to the indiscriminate editing of an outside source. Start a picture file. Photos, newspaper pictures, photocopies and the like can be tied directly into your lecture with an immediate reinforcement by simply holding them up as you speak.

To avoid breaking up the smooth flow of your lectures by having to stop and discipline one student, orient yourself toward certain code signals. Martha Hunt wrote on this in the <u>National Education Association Journal</u> in September, 1985. Snap your fingers and point; drift over in mid-sentence and wrap on his (her) desk; hover over the aloof student and raise your voice without breaking the train of thought.

Another thought on effective teaching and one that perhaps transcends lecturing and is applicable to all aspects of teaching is to avoid assumptions. Most children really do not question when you use a word that is foreign to them, when they simply do not grasp your meaning, or when they are lost. Be attuned to this, difficult though that may be. Slow down, set aside question times in which the questions come from you, give once-per-week in-class assignments so that you can meet with kids that you feel might be falling by the wayside. Face it, the basis of an effective lecture is that the listeners understand it.

Try to end each class on a positive note. End on a pun, the offering of a few minutes for them to "hang out," small talk, or a lecture-story in which you hang them in suspense, not telling the ending. This is sound advice for any teacher, administrator, businessman, coach, minister or whomever must deal with large groups of people.

It may sound trite, but as a final note on effective lecturing, it is advisable to "be yourself." Do not play-act or try to overtly copy from another style. Rita Dunn has discerned some thirty-six different teaching styles. You will fall into your own pattern and this is natural, but I also caution you to be sure that you are speaking to your audience. Temper your style to relate to your class. Thus, be yourself, but make it a self that is flexible enough to adapt to different audiences.

WHAT STUDENTS DO IN SCHOOL

John I. Goodlad in <u>A Study Of Schooling,</u> produced an elegant study on time allocation in American schools. He compared early elementary, upper elementary, junior high and senior high schools and the average amount of time spent on various school activities. I offer his findings with my editorial comments.

Individualized desk work seems to be most prevalent in elementary school - about 35 percent of the class time. This decreases to about 17 percent in high school and that, in my opinion, is about as it should be. Lecturing increases from 20 percent of the time in the elementary school years to only 27 percent of the time in high school. High school teachers should strive to increase lecture time as this is what students will most encounter in college.

Discussion and student participation stayed about the same throughout the school years, 10 percent / 11 percent of the class time, while taking tests rose from 2 percent / 3 percent of the elementary school's time to 6 percent of the high school's time. This seems acceptable and understandable. Let us not over-test the younger students and always remember that tests rob class time.

Audio-visual presentation fell from 5 percent / 7 percent of elementary school students' time to 3 percent of the high school students' time and physical exercise went from 7 percent to 18 percent. Perhaps an attempt should be made to raise physical education time in the lower grades as youths begin to encounter physical decline in terms of muscle flexibility and cardio-vascular conditioning from about age ten on. The 18 percent figure for the amount of time spent on physical activity in high schools might be a bit high, however.

The biggest criticism to be found in Goodlad's study, and he makes this point well, is that fully 12 percent of time in our schools is spent "getting organized." Better organization by teachers can cut this figure. Have your class planned and your materials organized. Have students pass out materials to save time and regularly assess you own practices so that you can make you class time more efficient.

Another important study on in-school time usage was prepared by The Association for Supervision and

Curriculum Development in the mid-1980's. Polling some
1500 elementary schools, they found that school time was
allocated in the following continuum, from least to
most:

```
        ART...................13 MINUTES
        MUSIC.................14 MINUTES
        PHYSICAL EDUCATION...15 MINUTES
        HEALTH...............22 MINUTES
        SCIENCE..............28 MINUTES
        SOCIAL STUDIES.......34 MINUTES
        MATHEMATICS..........52 MINUTES
        "OTHER"..............92 MINUTES
        ENGLISH.............100 MINUTES
```

Be advised that these statistics are based on the
average fourth-grader's day.

Much of this seems to be justifiable, but perhaps
there is too much time spent on "other," presumably
things like lunch, recess, administrative activities and
so on. Fully one-fourth of the school day, then, is
spent on non-academic or non-curricular work. To be ·
sure, outlets are necessary, but there must be greater
time-on-task consideration. It might be wise for each
teacher to individually examine his or her own time
allocation. Whatever the grade level, this can help in
terms of efficiency.

WHAT STUDENTS DO OUTSIDE OF SCHOOL

One might criticize this passage as the most
nebulous and individualized portion of this book, but I
would like to offer a few thoughts on student after-
school activities: homework, sports, and work.

In this age of increased academic demand being
placed upon students, there comes a point at which we
must assess how much, how often, and of what quality our
homework assignments are or should be. A recent study
by the Census Bureau offers some insights. They found
that the average high school student does some 6.5 hours
of homework per week (this is higher than the four hours
of homework per week cited by two large-scale studies
taken earlier and elsewhere); six percent of high school
youths studied as much as ten hours per week while 13
percent said that they did no homework at all.

The Census Bureau study also found that only 49
percent of American parents help their children with
their homework. My own experience has been that when

parents assist their children in their studies, or at least express some interest in their schooling, those students tend to perform better, take a greater interest in their education, and generally are of a higher academic caliber.

From the teacher's standpoint, it can be frustrating to deal with the number of assignments not turned in. Estimates vary according to the academic level of the class, but a statistical break-down of my own gradebook after the 1989-90 school year revealed that I graded 7,984 assigments out of 9383 given. Thus, simply put, students turned in and completed 85% of the work. Lower academic classes submitted 74% of the work on a year-long average. Interestingly, the senior honors students averaged a 94% turn-in rate for the first three marking periods and then dropped to 65% in marking period IV, thus manifesting true statistical "senior-itis." Ways to improve this figure are keeping classes small (so the students feel that they cannot hide), make sure that the work receives a grade and that it fits in with a particular lesson, see that there is some follow-up on the assignment in class discussion, see that assignments are scheduled routinely, and make sure that the work is relevant; never give "busy work."

Concerning sports, I can think of no better after-school activity. At the risk of sounding sophomoric, I believe that sports build notions of team responsibility, self-esteem, and commitment in ways that cannot be equaled elsewhere. Sports instill discipline in an unruly child. They help an introverted child emerge from his cocoon. Encourage your students to engage in school sports. Studies show that children in a sports season tend to budget their time better.

After school work is a touchy subject which depends upon many factors such as age, family income, college plans and so on. However, since so many students work after school, you will be certain to encounter the student who is over-committed to his job interests. Recent studies have shown that fifteen to twenty hours of work is optimal and limitational (U.S. News, 11/7/88). A simple phone call to parents or the employer can help relieve the problem. A firm line must be taken that school is the student's primary job. In the majority of cases, the parents or employer are unaware that the student is not fulfilling his academic demands and they usually side with you, the teacher.

MARKING PAPERS

I should be the last person telling anyone about marking papers as I am notoriously slow in returning corrected work to the students. However, I will offer a few comments about the ideal.

Each teacher will of course look at student work from different perspectives relative to both subject matter and personal tastes. I believe, however, that all of us owe it to our students, no matter what subject we teach, to correct misspelled words or syntax and grammar problems. On misspellings, it pays to correctly spell out the word rather than scrawl the traditional "sp" over the error. Few students ever take the time to look up a misspelled word even when you point it out to them. However, if the student has several misspelled words on a paper, I merely circle them, deduct five points, and return the paper for correction. When the student returns the corrected paper, he gets the points restored. I have even photocopied poor pages and sent them to English teachers for extra help. Even though my primary focus is in the area of history, I still feel that we, as teachers, share a common responsibility.

Make comments on papers. Studies have shown that annotated papers draw a positive response from students. Corrections, comments, and clarifications can be of more value than most us realize. Students appreciate knowing what is on your mind as you examine their work. This is especially true of subjective work like essays. If you down-grade the work, the student should know why. In making comments on papers, it is not inappropriate to jot down reminders such as missed assignments, important due dates and so forth. Furthermore, do not hesitate to praise students with positive comments in their papers. Studies bear out that this can decidedly boost student performance in the long run.

Try to return tests and quizzes as soon as possible. Remember that students are children and as such they need immediate reinforcement. It is difficult, to be sure, to get all of these essays graded that night and returned the next day, but it is, in an educational sense, worth the effort. One trick is that if you find you have difficulty meeting the deadline of immediate return, go over quizzes in class right after they are taken and collected. This way, the students get immediate feed-back. Granted, this is difficult with tests and security may be jeopardized, but quizzes can be handled in such a manner because they can easily be changed for students making them up later.

70

Send papers home. Referred to earlier, I reiterate here that when a student gives me no effort on a test, quiz, or homework, I make an effort to let his parents know about it by sending it home. Some parents do not care, but there are enough that do. The results can be positive.

Schedule your correcting time. To try to grade papers in between class preparation, lectures, office paperwork, parent conferences, and student help time, will afford you little time if any. I try to set aside three periods per week for correcting. I also grade two items of work (i.e. a set of tests and a set of homeworks) on each weekend. I find that this just about allows me to keep abreast. The key is to make this time inviolable - schedule nothing else into this correcting time otherwise the "To Be Corrected" folders just bulge and grow.

Paul Gagnon edited a colledtion of essays in a 1989 book entitled Historical Literacy. In it is quoted Ted Sizer's Horace's Compromise in which the former wrote, "Horace, says Sizer, is lucky. His suburban school assigns him five classes with a total of 120 students. His inner-city counterparts may have 175 or more. Good teachers want their students to write, but there is so little time to read their papers. It takes Horace ten hours to give each student's homework and compositions a five-minute look. Doing this twice a' week adds twenty hours to a "lucky" teacher's twenty-plus hours of class time - over forty hours are used up so far and we have not yet counted the hours needed for reading and selecting materials, for preparing for each of five classes five times a week, for administrative chores, department and school meetings, special academic or disciplinary problems after school, extra-curricular duties, meeting parents, counseling students, writing letters of recommendation. Nor have we yet touched upon keeping up with good books and articles in one's field or working with colleagues on curriculum, course design, and teaching methods, or monitoring practice teachers." (Gagnon, p. 253)

A hint on grading map assignments: make-up a transparency with the correctly located items on it. Your transparent map must be the identical copy of the work maps that the students use. When correcting, place your copy over theirs and the missed points will be easily discernible.

When grading test, I have found that a degree of consistency is ensured by grading section-by-section; all of the term section for the entire class and then all of the essay questions. Do this rather than student-by-student. You will find that your evaluative criterion is more uniform and that you look at answers rather than student names which serves to further enhance objectivity.

TEACHING TO WRITE ESSAYS

I believe that writing is an art. However, unlike many art forms, good narrative and analytical writing can be taught and cultivated. Most high school students have to be taught to write solid essays. It is a step-by-step process that unfolds over the course of a semester, if not a year.

First off, lay two ground rules - one for yourself and one for your students. Tell yourself that your students have no idea of what constitutes a good essay. Starting from that assumption, you can begin the step-by-step process. Secondly, tell your students that you want specific data on essays and that they will obtain points for their work only if that specific information is included. Some teachers call this the "meter is running" approach. Points are awarded only when specific data appears in the essay.

On the first test of the year, I give only one essay question and I will tell the students exactly what it is. By way of clarification, I stress to the reader that this process is for a developmental or under-achieving class, not the above-average grouping of students that makes us all look so good. Next I will outline on the board what I will be looking for in the essay. Tell them how you grade - what they have to include for the essay to be acceptable and earn points. Emphasize the outlining concept while you are presenting it - this is critical toward writing specific, material-oriented essays. I then tell them that in their study they should prepare an essay outline and this should be committed to memory - it is like a skeleton that must be fleshed out on the test. Warn the students that if they do not include a portion of the outlined material, or if they fail to explain it, or if they fail to employ narrative format, they will lose points.

Once the first test is taken, hopefully you will be pleased at what you find in their essays. If students show an effort, but still have not done well on the essay - and there will be several - give it back to them for correcting, filling in and filling out. Also, it is a good policy to have students who did well on the essay read theirs aloud to the class for comparison sake.

On the second test and on perhaps all subsequent tests, depending upon the students' learning abilities, I will "think out loud" with the class, asking them what they think the essays might be. This helps them identify essay-type material, the large blocks of material that can be analyzed, compared, contrasted and synthesized. From feedback I have gotten from returning college students, this practice does seem to help.

Essay writing must be practiced; it must not be reserved for tests alone. Do not be deluded into thinking that end-of-chapter text questions will help the students formulate good essays. In most cases these answers are copied, ill-considered, and/or randomly scrawled. Assign work like "You Are There" essays which I will describe later, or editorial writing, "Judgment of History" essays or problem assignments in areas of directed research. These build specific essays.

Another idea to enhance writing practice is to have students write on issues that they can relate to emotionally - divorce, abortion, politics, crime and so on. They will get the feel of putting specific ideas on paper.

I have already mentioned my thoughts on test-construction as it pertains to essays. Most of the time I do not directly tell them what the essays will be (telling them generally occurs only in the beginning of the process). On subsequent tests I have them select two out of three essays given on the test to answer. Have them select the two essays that they feel strongest about individually.

By utilizing the outlining method, essay identification, and drill concepts, I think that you will find that you receive better essays from your pupils.

I realize that I have not tied in analysis. Aside from compare and contrast questions, we cannot expect the majority of our high school students to postulate new, innovative ideas or original research. We can, and should, ask for their original thoughts in term papers, reports, and editorials, but test essays should be of material orientation. Their knowledge of specific material is what is being evaluated - pin them down to that.

Let me tie in a component often overlooked in the teaching of writing: reading. Studies show that reading enhances writing. Certainly it helps broaden vocabulary and the general scope of the mind, but reading also helps in the learning of idea-transmission, sentence structure, paragraph composition, and so forth. Keep your students reading as well as writing.

E. D. Hirsch has addressed the problem of what he calls, in his book of the same title, "Cultural Literacy" and he decries the decline of such literacy in American youth as a failing of the education system. He refers to the essential concepts, terms of reference, names, events and phrases that every American needs to know to effectively communicate in American society. In his 1987 bestseller he rails at what he sees as American youth becoming "cultural illiterates." Accepting or rejecting this thesis can best be left to your own judgment, but it merits consideration from an education standpoint; and having your students read, read, read, will help overcome communication as well as writing deficiencies.

And finally, try to avoid giving writing assignments as punishment work. Logically, this is counter-productive to the entire process of teaching writing. Students will come to associate writing with drudgery and punishment.

PLANNING LESSONS...

Teaching can be relatively simple, but it requires the mastery of two basic concepts - acquisition of knowledge and transmission of knowledge. We have discussed the transmission of knowledge in our segment on effective lecturing.

Whatever your major or field of study, most certainly the acquisition of knowledge is occurring right now. Much of what you are learning in those classes pertaining to your major will form the basis of your formative lesson plans when you teach. Hence, do not discard your notebooks.

However, you will find yourself refining the process and material as your career unfolds. Notwithstanding your course's text, you will find that your early lesson plans, basically regurgitation of your college notes, will be broadened, changed, and updated as you read, take further course work and graduate study, and most importantly, formulate your own ideas. Thus, your lessons five and ten years from now will be vastly different from what they will be in your first year of teaching. You will find that as you teach new courses in your career, the first lesson plans are but explorations in that you will transmit the little you know and amplify this later. (I have often felt retrospective sorrow for the students who take the class with me when I am teaching it for the first time). You will synthesize information from a variety of sources, but most important is your outside reading. There truly is need for the good teacher to be a continuing student. If you stop learning when you receive your Bachelors Degree, you will have enough ammunition to teach, but not enough to sustain. And to stop learning is to stop teaching effectively.

Perhaps an aside, but I have always felt that it is important for the teacher to obtain a Master Degree in his academic field rather than in a general area such as education, supervision, or administration. Bluntly stated, the latter areas are simply too watered down and nebulous to be of practical value to your classroom teaching. True, you may have upper-echelon career goals, but then you are not teaching, either.

I have thus far discussed two methods of preparing a lesson - the verbatim/regurgitation method and the synthesis method. Do not completely dismiss the verbatim method even after you have spent several years teaching. You may wish to use a particularly enthralling lecture by one of your professors in its entirely. To do this, simply reproduce the lecture notes, pass out copies, and present the data. Please, just credit the professor with the material. I suggest the note copies to ensure a bit more accuracy in your presentation of the borrowed material. As regards the synthesis lesson, you will find that this method is used often in classes in which you have no formal course work. I majored in European History in college and found myself teaching the histories of Latin America and Africa in my first year. Yes, it took a lot of reading; and yes, this is all too common.

You have gotten into a good habit while in college - that of underlining and annotating your books. This actually makes your once-read books more valuable than a new copy right off the store shelf. Continue this habit. And after you have read a book that contains some useful data for a lesson you will present in class, jot down the notes into your lesson plans. You will find that you re-type your lessons about once every three or four years this way, but they get better and better as time goes on. I once heard a teacher say that they did not have time to read books... such a person is incomplete in so many ways.

Sources to be used in preparing lessons include of course books, periodicals, articles, handouts and lesson plans from colleagues who have taught the same course, newspaper, television shows - virtually any dispenser of information that you can lay your hands on. Do not be proud; steal everything. Once the acquisition of a data base is secured, refine it through further reading and study.

...AND LESSON PLANS

I have included a few copies of sample lesson plans earlier in this book. Note that some are very detailed and some are sketchy. You will find that the longer you teach, a certain irony emerges - the lesson plans become more sketchy, but the amount of information imparted becomes more detailed. The change is natural - you know your material better.

A variety of lesson plans can be utilized. I prefer a single notesheet to face me and this lies atop a compilation of all lectures relative to that particular course. This enables me to maintain a degree of flow, past and present. Note that I will have readings cited if they are to be used and if I am using the over-head projector, then the overlay transparency serves as the lecture notes.

As noted earlier you may wish to utilize a spiral notebook or 5 x 7" index cards. I have suffered through courses where the teacher's notes are the textbook and together we read it aloud or work page by page, chapter by chapter. This probably does ensure an exact coverage of the course content, but it stifles a class, ruins spontaneity, and very often proves infernally boring.

These are the practical lesson plans that you will actually use. You have by now learned about "behavioral objectives," "performance goals," and so on. These are fine, and most administrations in schools require some sort of formal lesson plans. Their real value, as I see it, lies in the planning. With the office-mandated lesson plans, which I will not go into here as you have been bludgeoned to boredom with these in your present education classes and they vary so greatly from school to school, you can look ahead to the week's planning and lay out a strategy. They are of benefit, but they are over-emphasized. What I described at the onset - the practical, in-class lecture notes - is what you will find most useful and most used. On the following page, I have included a copy of the weekly lesson plans that I use; these are not lecture notes, but rather planning forms that the central office would require. As mentioned, they do serve to help plan out the week and it is necessary that the administrative offices are aware of what is going on in the classroom, but they have little utilitarian value beyond that.

Let me caution about keeping photocopies of all lesson plans. I once lost the notes to a valuable lesson and swore that I would henceforth maintain a central file of all lesson plans. I then discovered something. This is the stuff from which books are derived. The compilation of the lessons for a particular course makes the skeleton for a book. I suppose that this is how general texts in history, science, math and so on are written. The teacher(s) merely flesh out their lesson plans into a textbook. Maybe someday....

LESSON PLANS	WEEK OF: Dec.9,1985	Teacher: R.Trimble
ANTHROPOLOGY Pd.2	WORLD HISTORY Pd.4	U.S.HISTORY I Pd.7

test review
collect ch.7
cover family structure
  diagramming and go into
  geneology
  handouts
	filmstrip on Russ.Rev.
	--use w/handout on items
	to look for - q/a
	collect at end of class
	emphasize:two revs.
	     Lenin
	     Bolsheviks
	
	text:ch.15
		Crime Unit: ct.
		system, plea
		bargainingcapital
		punishment,argument
		 pro/con
		
		collect 2C case
		studies and go
		over,if time

TEST on culture,
society
	Inter-War Era:
	Age of Dictators
	define fascism
	a.reinforce Hitler rise
	b.Stalin:purges,
	  collectivization,
	  indsutrialization
		go over case
		studies
		issues:gun
		control,prison
		reform - pass out
		articles and
		discuss after
		reading them

Film: The Hunters (Bushmen of the Kalahari) pt.1	c.Mussolini d.Franco:Spanish Civil War assign ch.questions text: chs.18,19	terms due assign editorials for Monday allow students time to work on assignments, library use, teacher-time for tutoring
film (above) pt.2	individual time: assignments,see teacher, library,read discuss Oral History project	1.prep for speaker 2.review for test 3.filmstrip:crime
discuss film - contrast lifestyles with Nanook of North film discuss term paper progress;collect outlines return corrected work assign ch.9	Unit:WWII-Europe a.origins/causes b.assign maps c.collect chs.18,19 d.quik-quiz	Guest Speaker: Susan Alois- Mon.Cty.Pros.Offic topic:NJ Ct.System

78

STRUCTURING A COURSE

At the time of this writing, I am about to enter my eighteenth year of teaching. Over that tenure, I can remember only two years when I did not have a new course to teach. The point of this parable is that in a sense, we become new teachers every year.

Given a course assignment, you can count yourself lucky if you are offered a course syllabus or outline. In most cases you will want to prepare your own or even make modifications of the one given you. This is understandable as you are the teacher and you have your own interpretations, slants, presentation modes, and theories. In structuring a course, first think of what you would like the students to do. You may want a final exam, a written paper, a series of tests and quizzes, an oral report or whatever else helps transmit the knowledge. Be aware of the type of class and the type of student who generally takes the class as this will help you make your decision about course requirements. You can make modifications, but this is a starting point.

The next step is to consider what you want to cover. Work up an outline for the entire course. Plug in student requirements. Add a list of suggested readings and projects. This your rough draft. The next step is to solicit input from colleagues, preferably those who might have taught the course before, and from supervisors. At the very least, pause to reflect upon the outline yourself - do not dash off to the copy machine with an ill-considered rough draft; this facet of the planning is certainly the most important aspect of your pre-teaching. Are there any films that you would like to show? Any speakers that you would like to bring in? Flesh out the skeleton syllabus.

Now it is time to re-type, run off, and distribute to the students.

I like to keep a copy of each course syllabus in my folder containing the teaching notes for the entire course. Some teachers tend to over-organize and make voluminous course outlines, even adding lecture dates. This tends to lock you in too much. A concise overview is usually sufficient. Besides, putting dates down insures another re-typing next semester. When first teaching the course it is too difficult to accurately determine the length of time you will spend on each topic anyway.

A course outline provides structure to your course and students, but above all, it ensures that you are prepared and organized as you present a course for the first time.

Selecting a textbook for your course can be problematic. Unless you have some familiarity with the types of texts and offerings available then you may have to rely upon the recommendation of a colleague or supervisor. However, let us assume that you can, in fact, select your own text. Book publishers liberally offer their wares. They can be contacted either through your supervisor or through your librarian; either person will be able to provide you with telephone numbers. Ask for copies of what they have to offer in your particular subject area.

Sitting down with several candidate texts that you may choose from, first consider the academic level of your student population. If they are college-bound, give them a college-type text with end-of-chapter bibliographies. Then you should teach the course in the college-like manner. If your class is of junior high or freshmen caliber, then you should look for a text with end-of-chapter questions, highlighting, etc.

Other criterion to consider when looking for a textbook are these:

a) How well does the text fit the material you plan to teach?

b) Is the text going to be understandable for your student clientele?

c) Are there sufficient maps and diagrams?

d) Will you need a book of supplemental readings?

e) Is the text current enough? Note that in some classes such as Social Problems, Environmental Issues, and Current World Affairs, a text might be inappropriate and a better reading source would be articles that you obtain, a newspaper, or a newsmagazine. Refer back to my thoughts on putting together your own book of supplemental readings.

  f) Is the book sufficiently highlighted and readable for your students, considering their academic level?

  g) What are the author's credentials? This might be important for higher academic classes.

  h) Will you need paperback or hardbound? If your course is of current material, then a paperbound text might be better. You cannot expect more than four or five course usages from a paperback and by that time the course may need updating anyway.

  i) Consider the "Fog Index." In a brilliant piece, Gayle White, staff writer for the "Atlanta Constitution" defined this. Select a one-hundred word sample from each text. Calculate the average sentence length and also count the number of three-or-more-syllable words you see. Multiply the sum by 0.4. The product is the Fog Index rating and this roughly equals the grade level of schooling that the reader will need to comprehend the piece.*

  j) How easily do the chapters lend themselves to outlining and question-answering?

  k) And perhaps the most important component, consider your gut reaction to the text - do you like it?

  Initially, book need not be read in its entirety; simply peruse it with a specific eye to the table of contents, the index, and the supplementation.

THE FIRST DAY OF SCHOOL

  Here it is at last: your first day on the job, facing a group of sun-tanned faces who have mixed feelings about being there and are quietly sizing you up with every gesture you make. For some it is a frightening experience while for others it is greeted with a sense of drudgery and inevitability as the question is tacitly understood, "Where did the summer go?" Whatever the feeling is, consider that this is one of the plusses of the teaching field - the fresh start

---

*This is but one simple method of determining the reading level for a text. There are many more, including the Fry Readability Graph (Journal of Reading, April, 1968); consult your Guidance Department or Child Study Team for other assessment programs and devices.

that occurs every year. Also realize that your
feelings, whatever they may be - antipathy or
anticipation - are the same feelings the kids have.

I like to prepare a checklist for the first day of
each school year. Aside from the list of duties that
the school will provide such as enrollment, health data
cards, school policy changes, distribution of student
handbooks, fire bell procedures, and so on, I like to
use my own list of things that I know must get done for
my own classes.

My typical list would include things like the
following:
- a) textbooks
- b) Student Study Guides
- c) any assignment master listings
- d) course outlines
- e) classroom rules and procedures
- f) reading lists
- g) pre-tests
- h) course proficiencies (if required)
- i) 3 x 5" cards containing student name,
     address, phone number and parents' name
     if different from their own
- j) course requirements

If the checklist takes more than one day to
complete, which it should, then so be it. These are
fundamentally important things that must not be omitted.

During these first few days the basic classroom
atmosphere will be established. The theory has been set
forward by educational theorist T. Roger Taylor that the
basic classroom atmosphere, as modeled by the teacher,
is established within three days in the elementary
school classroom and ten days in the high school
classroom.

There are two divergent approaches which can be used
here. I have heard teachers say that they like to come
down hard with iron-fisted discipline and then relax as
the school year goes on. On the other hand, there are
teachers who like to win students over with an open,
friendly tone. Both have their place and must be
determined by, a) your own personality type, b) the
openness or restrictiveness you like in your classroom,
and c) the students themselves. In explanation of item

one, be yourself. To play-act either the matron or the charlatan invites inconsistency. It has often been said that kids can easily spot the phony in an adult and I think that this is true. As for the second, I like an open, easy air in the classroom, so I try to be less restrictive. I will allow a blurted-out answer and crack a few jokes on opening days, setting the mood I want. However, if you have a class of reputed trouble-makers, then your discipline had better prevail from day one. Never pre-judge a class, but try not to be caught off-guard when it comes to a class of students. Very often, you can tell the personality of a class even as they walk into the room. Also consider the size of the class. The bigger the class, then by necessity, the tighter the discipline and atmosphere must be.

Be organized that first day. Nothing will hurt you more in the eyes of your students than a fumbling, forgetful approach.

Oh yes, first year teachers - remember the Pledge of Allegiance. Chances are that you have not said it much during the past four years of college and you may have forgotten the words. Seventeen years ago - I remember it well - I had my lists, my handouts, everything. I had it all together. But I forgot the words to the Pledge of Allegiance. The bubble burst....

TEACHING FRESHMEN/TEACHING SENIORS

What a difference! While both can be refreshing, both can be challenging in their own unique way. There is a need for a varied approach between these two student age-groups.

Freshmen need structure and humor. Since they are at the peak of that wonderful twelve -fourteen age bracket in which everything that does not conform to their sense of propriety is considered "stupid," a class of ninth graders should be given guidelines such as notebook checks, notesheets, weekly quizzes, text question homework assignments, chapter outlining, and so on. These give direction and purpose. Freshmen, for the most part, cannot handle such open-ended chores as professor-like lectures and research papers. Because I want my freshmen to get a dose of high school reality (i.e. - academic demand) and because their assignments are more direct and simple, I tend to give more homework to freshmen, though much of it tends to be objective, factual and straight-forward. My freshmen get chapter questions, short-answer work and so on in greater volume than my upper classmen might. Deep, penetrating and provocative questions do not seem to work well with freshmen either. Their responses are more often based on emotion and "being cool" rather than reflective, critical analysis.

Another point is that freshmen are often less inhibited. They will ask more questions; they will stray from your intended lecture topics and they will perform better in role-playing type work.

As for lecturing, leaven your talks with puns, poor jokes, and wisecracks. Freshmen seen to especially relish such low-grade humor. They find it difficult to sit through a full-blown lecture. The attention span of ninth-graders is probably not much more than that of sixth graders. Jokes snap the wandering mind back to your focus.

My first dose of freshmen mentality came after years of teaching higher caliber seniors and juniors. Not accustomed to teaching down to their level, I was stopped in mid-sentence with, "Mr. Trimble, Freddy's passing notes about me." Yes, ninth graders are different from seniors.

Seniors - what four years can do! With highly motivated students there may actually be little change as they continue to perform at a solid level throughout their high school career. However, the disaffected student seems to lose much of his clownishness by his senior year. He may still be listless, careless, and failing but he is often times not the obnoxious, immature brat he was four years earlier.

In dealing with seniors, first assess their intellectual capabilities. Remember that we are dealing with near adults, many of whom are nearing the end of their academic careers and by this time it is apparent to all who has it and who does not. If you can, try to teach your seniors on a more college-like level, or at least give them more college-like assignments. They must have essays, abstract thinking, and conceptual work as opposed to the objective/factual approach you use with your freshmen. Your lectures can be more academic; your overall presentation less oriented toward structured data memorization. You can rely upon seniors to cover certain phases of the course content on their own by giving them research assignments into directed areas through labs, critical-thought essays, and so on. This approach can be problematic for freshmen.

This is not intended to mean that every senior can handle the more cerebral approach. If you have a class of seniors whose academic prowess is that of a freshmen class, then modify the college-like approach. Even with a weak senior class, however, I would still not teach in the identical fashion that I would normally use with a strong freshmen class. Seniors will soon be out on their own, be it in the work-a-day world or in college. It matters little if they remember the composition of the Triple Entente or the atomic weight of mercury; it does matter if they can write a coherent essay, express their thoughts clearly, and make logical, intelligent decisions.

It may sound obvious, but know for certain who your seniors are. Sometime during the first days of class, double-check who your seniors are. This can save you considerable embarrassment later in the spring when it comes time for their graduation and the office wants to know their status.

Keep your senior class loose. Allow for a free flow of ideas. Have fun with them. They are almost your peers.

TEACHING THE SMALL CLASS AS WELL AS THE LARGE CLASS

There is a bit of a controversy within education circles as to the validity of the claim that smaller classes - twenty students or less - are more conductive to the educational process. Do kids learn more and/or better in smaller classes? To me, there is no controversy - students do learn better and learn more in smaller classes. Both common sense and repeated studies have shown this. Those who contend that class size means nothing are those who are usually in administrative positions and like the larger classes because of budgetary considerations. Larger classes are cheaper.

Stony Brook University in New York wanted to see if the sizes of their calculus classes in 1984 had any impact on student success. When they dropped the class size - to 35! - failures declined by 21 percent and A-grades rose by 21 percent. The National Association of Secondary School Principals recommended in 1983 that class size not exceed twenty students.

The National Education Association, in an admittedly self-serving yet still significant position paper, found that with smaller classes teachers were better able to diagnose individual student problems, discipline was better and that students committed fewer aggressive acts. Teachers were more innovative; there was greater student involvement in the learning process; there was greater interaction between students and between students and teacher; and teachers modified questioning methods to better facilitate student understanding. In addition, students enjoyed the class better as a whole, teachers increased the number of assignments given, there was more creative thinking, and "Students achieve better in nearly all skills and subjects, but especially in language, reading, mathematics, physical and mechanical skills, science, social studies, spatial relationships, and reasoning."

Studies show that when class size increases from twenty students to twenty-five, there is little impact, but when the class size goes beyond twenty-five, there are dramatic negative results.

The superiority of the small class is logical. Teachers can more easily assess the individual interests, abilities, weaknesses, skills, and personal background of each student. The result is a better learning environment as we approach the ideal teacher-student ratio of one-to-one. Granted, the latter is economically unrealistic, but it is indisputably the most efficient learning atmosphere. Were this not so, then why would private tutoring be of the premium that it is?

As a teacher, you will teach in both settings - large classes as well as small ones. Both must be handled differently, although both can be equally rewarding.

With larger classes, the overall presentation must be more structured and discipline must be tighter. You may have to resort to seating charts, notesheets, and so forth. However, larger classes have the manpower to enable you to assign and do large-scale projects more easily. Things like debates, polls, forums, and community projects can more easily be done with the larger classes.

Smaller classes allow for a more personable, relaxed approach. More socio-dramas, writing assignments, open-ended discussion, oral reports, brainstorming sessions, and so on can be done. With smaller classes, it is not always necessary that you stand before them in traditional teacher positioning. You may wish to enhance the personal atmosphere by sitting down with the students in a round-table setting and teach from there; you may wish to take them outside on warm days. You can meet with individual students more easily. Attentively, the smaller classes will stay with you longer, allowing you to present more material if you wish. Each student feels that he is less able to hide in a smaller class. Similarly, because you will move more quickly through your scheduled curriculum with a smaller class, you can supplement, detail, and vary your overall presentations more effectively.

Simply put, it seems to me that it takes more knowledge of the course content and more teaching artistry to work with the smaller class. It takes more of a disciplinarian to work with the larger class. The complete teacher will be faced with both class sizes, so he/she must be able to adapt to both.

TEACHING HONORS CLASSES

It is appropriate at this juncture to put down a few words about teaching Advanced Placement or honors classes as they tend to be smaller in size and a bit unique in terms of the challenges they present.

Honors students must be taught in the college mode. Lectures, essays, concepts and analytical thought must be the criteria you employ. I have found that oral presentations are a must. In teaching history and English classes on the honors level, give students as many books to read and review as can be possible; expose them to the top minds in the field.

As a general rule, I lecture to my Honors History class three times per week - as in a college course. I like to hold one day aside for recitations or oral presentations of short pieces of related reading material that have been passed out the week before. These might be works by contemporary thinkers, primary source material, analytical briefs, and so on. Such works is considered crucial to successfully teaching top college-bound students by many teachers of Advanced Placement courses. It also tends to help prepare them for the Advanced Placement test with its short analytical excerpts. I will set aside one day for seat work, during which time I will meet with individual students to assist them with papers, readings, allow students to go to the library, etc.

Select a college text for these students. A simple hint is whether or not the text has run-of-the-mill questions at the end of the chapters or if it has a bibliography. Usually the latter indicates a more advanced-level text. If still unsure, talk to colleges themselves to find out what they use (call their bookstore or department chairmen); talk to colleagues in your school or others and do not forget to talk to graduated students to see what texts are currently being used. Have your students employ outlining techniques much as they would if they were underlining a text that they owned.

It may be esoteric, but I will say that I like my advanced history students to be familiar with key historians, schools of history, and "mistakes historians make" in writing and researching papers. In short, I give them an overview of the dreaded Historiography course - the bane of many a history major.

Like it or not, we should give consideration to preparing them for the Advanced Placement test in their field. Although it should not be the end-all, be-all evaluation of your course and teaching, it is only fair to help your students along when they shell out so much money to take the test. Preparing for the test can come from the basic assignments you present throughout the school year - the recitations, maps and analytical briefs. Add in statistical analysis as that seems to figure prominently, too. Teach them to write good essays. Provide them with copies of previously given tests by photocopying those administered each year or those supplied by Educational Testing Services. I assure you that this is perfectly legal. The rest is up to the student. A big factor in their success, however, will be whether or not the year they take the Advanced Placement test is their first year of studying the course material. Particularly with the tests in the sciences and in European History it is difficult for students to score well if they have only had one year of study in the particular discipline. English and U.S. History students seem to fare better as theirs is a more protracted study.

I have used the terms Advanced Placement (A.P.) and Honors courses inter-changably, yet there is difference. Honors classes, I believe, should be more analytical and critical. Successful A.P. courses tend to be drill-oriented and mechanical in their approach. Both, however, must address higher thinking levels rather than names, dates and facts.

Do not be intimidated by the prospect of teaching the cream of the student crop. Without doubt, you will have to know your stuff and be familiar with key literature and current studies. In all probability, the teaching of these upper level courses will be given to a more veteran colleague anyway. It is my firm belief that because the teacher of an honors course in high school is essentially teaching a college course to college kids, he should possess at least a Masters Degree in his subject field. Although this is not always possible given the limitations of a faculty in what is perhaps a small school, it definitely helps the educational process.

Discipline problems are few and the kids are highly motivated, but there is a bit of pressure on you as the teacher to know your field. There might even be some misguided pressure to have you ensure that the students do well on the Advanced Placement test. Students, parents, and administrators can expect the former, not especially the latter. Consider it an honor then, to teach an honors course. This will probably end up being your best class of the day.

A few words on teaching the college student might be appropriate, although I must admit that as of this writing, I am only beginning what I hope is a long career as an adjunct professor. I have found that too many professors enter an isolated world and become carried away with formal lecturing, forgetting or even disdaining basic concepts of classroom motivation.

All of the concepts of effective lecturing, varied classroom presentation, and so forth that I have cited earlier certainly have applicability for the college professor. Although weekly homework assignments and quizzes, so important to the high school course, should be minimized in college, certainly oral presentations of papers and readings are appropriate. I believe that a final exam is a must also. Students simply learn more when a final exam is given - it culminates, reinforces, and ties together an entire course. Since time is often at a premium for college instructors, try take-home mid-terms or finals. Deep, reflective-thought essays can be a solid tool in the collegiate educational process. These also free up your time for you to discuss more of your subject. On the other hand, it forces the student to integrate sources, express ideas, write critically, and demonstrate understanding.

I have seen films used very well in college classes, but be selective here.

Avoid reading your lecture material! Why do college teachers do this? How many times have you attended a lecture and the professor reads from a paper he or she wrote? This simply does not have the same educational impact as a lively, animated lecture. And finally, in most college classes, some written analytical assignment is necessary. It could be a book report or research paper, but students should have the opportunity to express themselves - and perhaps even add to the body of knowledge - about a particular issue.

In teaching my college classes, I like to present a weekly packet of handouts which includes supplemental and/or current readings, a reference map or graph data, and so forth. The feedback from my students suggests that they do find these packets helpful. But one student jokingly noted that another former pupil observed, "Oh, you must have Trimble and his handouts from Hell."

TEACHING THE CLASSIFIED STUDENT

I may be straying from my area of expertise here, but with the current trend toward "mainstreaming" impaired or handicapped children into the regular classroom, a few words might be appropriate. First off, any school counseling staff, child study team, or guidance department worth it's salt should let you know of any such student in your class and of his or her limitations and needs. If they do not inform you directly, then you should consult them. Their professional advice is the best counsel you can obtain. Calling parents directly for advice on how to handle their classified children can be risky business. One can never be sure how they are going to react to your

inquiries. Do so only as a last resort or upon
professional counsel.

Depending upon the impairment, the adjustments you
make may range from the simple to the complex. It may
be only a seating change for a child with a visual or
hearing problem. It may mean that a teacher aid is
assigned to that particular student in your room if the
problem is acute.

Whatever the case, make the student feel involved in
the class. Be sure to talk with the student one-to-one
so that you can make certain assessments on your own.
Be positive with the child in as many ways as possible.*
Be attuned to comments from the other students in the
class - kids can be cruel, so squash any unnecessary and
unkind remarks. Speak to the student(s) uttering such
barbs in no uncertain terms.

Some of these impaired students have tremendous
intellectual capability, but because of their
impairment they cannot actuate their academic potential.
Draw them out in any way possible. Give oral tests
either in lieu of or in addition to regularly
assigned work. Perhaps specialized texts are needed
(i.e. - large print, braille, or taped readings). These
latter items can be obtained from your counseling team.
You can administer tests on tape or reproduce them on
large-screen transparencies.

Certain materials might be available from state and
county departments of education, the Department of
Health, Education and Welfare in Washington, or from the
American Printing House for the Blind, 1839 Frankfort
Avenue, Louisville, Kentucky, 40206.

Whatever the case, three ingredients are needed
from you as the teacher: flexibility, understanding,
and care. You will derive a great sense of satisfaction
from seeing these students achieve. Similarly, by not
caring, you can damage your reputation, and the
school's, beyond repair.

---

*Ten Steps for Motivating Reluctant Learners, ERA Press,
Amherst, Mass., 01004

HOME TUTORING

Some teachers view this as a burden, but home instruction can be one of the more rewarding aspects of teaching, both in terms of monetary gain as well as professional satisfaction.

When a student is to be out of school due to an extended illness or other incapacitation, he or she goes on home instruction. Either the parent or the school will contact interested teachers and the work will be in your general area of instruction. The first step is to let it be known, by informing the main office or the Guidance Office, that you wish to be contacted for such jobs.

Once getting the home instruction assignment, make an appointment with the child and parents. Try to make this appointment time firm and set on a weekly or semi-weekly basis so that others, including colleagues and the student himself, will not infringe on this time.

Two types of home instruction emerge at the point - supplemental help and replacement teaching. In the case of supplemental help, it is usually because the student is failing and needs to pass. Close contact with the classroom teacher is necessary here as you will need to know assignments, tests, papers, due dates, etc. In most cases the student in this type of home instruction simply has not been doing assigned work. Rather than be fearful of such "he must pass - you teach" cases, it is actually a bit easier than the home tutoring I refer to as replacement teaching. During your assigned hour(s) you will basically work on homework with the child. If no particular homework assignment is due and upcoming, then test him orally to determine strengths and weaknesses or have him work on supplemental assignments that he might turn in for extra credit. Use your imagination. On a cautionary vein, there will be times when you may not receive proper or sufficient communication from the classroom teacher, particularly if you are working with a student from another school. If this is the case, get on the phone; have the parents call or contact the proper supervisors. Sometimes you will have to twist an arm.

The second type of home instruction is replacement teaching. Since the child is out of school, you are teaching him in lieu of the classroom teacher. What I give my pupils in this type of home tutoring is a stripped-down version of the classroom work. There are no filmstrips, no guest speakers, no classroom study time - only lecture and note presentation, pure and simple. The student has a week's worth of notes in one hour or two. It can be done, bearing in mind that one-on-one you can cover material so much faster. Work off a specially prepared ditto if need be. Then, if time permits, work with him on homework and other assignments. For grading purposes, I give a short oral pop-quiz each week based upon the previous week's notes. This sets the tone for the upcoming lesson and forces the child to review before you come. Furthermore, I tell them that since they generally have more time, I pile on the homework. They could receive more homework than the class is actually getting. Most students are usually so bored by sitting home that I hear few, if any, complaints.

Give these students your home telephone number. As anathema as that may sound, the home instruction student may need to contact you for appointment changes, questions regarding his work, and so on. Remember that he does not have the immediate access to you that a student in school does.

Keep records. Once the child returns to school, an accurate record of material covered, homework assigned, and grades earned will greatly help the classroom teacher. Some teachers will tell you that they only want a composite average for the child's work while others may wish to plug certain grades into certain areas within their scheme of grade assessment. Plus a written record looks more professional and covers yourself.

I have had students graduate from "Trimble High." We both laugh about it now, but we both know that when they graduated, the time spent on home instruction made the difference. I had one young man wink at me on the graduation line after receiving his diploma. We both knew why. What a satisfying feeling for any teacher.

TEACHING TO WRITE THE TERM PAPER

To write effective, coherent term papers, I feel that there is a progression that must begin in the junior high school years and ultimately culminate in the junior or senior year. To ask our seniors to compose original research and thesis papers is generally unrealistic. What we can expect is the well-constructed, lucid, fluent, and presentable research paper. In the college years, the research paper can,

with erudition and skill, develop into the thesis paper*
or one with original research.

In the eighth and ninth grades, students should be
exposed to some degree of directed research. They must
get the feel of source material and their utilization.
Biographies are easy starting points. Have students
turn in five hundred-word research papers on
Shakespeare, Churchill or Darwin. With older people
such as students, but of poorer academic caliber who
have yet to learn applied research, assign topics that
are interesting yet not that hard to find. Try battles,
catastrophes, or events. Try science reports on
anatomical systems or famous scientists. Have them list
sources; allow the use of encyclopedias. Show them what
data will be needed for a bibliography and have them
list that, too. This should be sufficient to get their
feet wet.

My general rule for the junior-senior research paper
is to give them a date two months hence, stipulating one
month for research and one month for writing. I ask for
ten typed pages with a bibliography and footnotes and/or
endnotes. I ask that no encyclopedias be cited in the
bibliography and I always give out a listing of
suggested research topics.

The topic selection is crucial. Students tend to
pick areas that are too broad. We must take the time to
teach the topic selection. I use an analogy that the
longer the topic title, the more defined the topic is.
Cite this example:

The World
History of the World
History of the Western World
History of the Western World Since 1900
History of Blond-haired People in the Western World
Since 1900

...and so on...the students get the point. Ask that
their topics be written on 3 x 5" cards so that you can
list some suggested sources for them. Do this and
return the cards.

---

*We must be careful of the terms we use here - all too
often "thesis papers" are generic terms when in fact, a
thesis paper sets to prove a pre-conceived theme or
message and involves the usage of any and all literary
evidence. This takes a person of letters, not a high
school senior, and it really only encompasses a small,
esoteric brand of research.

About one month before the paper is due, ask that the students submit an outline of their paper's contents. Not much more than a table of contents, this helps stimulate some early research and effort. Moreover, the corrections and comments that you make on these outlines can help re-direct their research, prevent a major mistake before it happens in print, or fill in data apparently missing from the paper. To me, the outlines are so critical that to stimulate their being done, I tell the students that I will even accept them late without late penalty (I tell the delinquent ones this after the due date for the outlines has arrived). I am telling them that it is better to get these outlines in for my perusal than to omit them altogether.

I offer to review rough drafts and, although few students take me up on this, it does seem to help those that do.

As for the research techniques, I do not specify that the 3 x 5" card system used by many English Departments be done. Nor do I grade the cards or the rough draft as some teachers do. I like to allow some degree of academic freedom for the students to employ their own research techniques. I do show them the 3 x 5" card method if they have not already been drilled in it and I do teach from my Student Study Guide as to the notebook method of research that I personally use. As noted earlier, I have included a copy of that study guide in this volume. How you handle the research technique is up to you. Do not be afraid to show them what has worked for you.

A word to your students on footnotes and bibliographies will probably be in order even with upper level classes. They invariably want to know what to footnote. I tell them that if they are in doubt, footnote it. More specifically, I came up with an acronym some years back that seems to fit: SQUAN (the nickname for Manasquan High School) - Statistics, Quotations, and Unusual Author Notations. Use this one or devise your own, but it does help the students identify what should be footnoted.

In short, term papers are taught. There must be a progression to the teaching; students must be coached along the way. Make no presumptions that because they might be advanced students they can know it all. The method I describe has worked for me and I have been pleased with the results.

SELF-ANALYSIS: A FORGOTTEN COMPONENT

Many of us are steeped in the tradition that the Teacher Is Always Right; once we become teachers we had better admit to ourselves that we are not always right. Thus the need for self-analysis and self-evaluation. It is important to evaluate the ways we teach and how we come across to the students, and search for more effective and efficient ways of doing things.

With the advent of automatic test-scoring machines and their item-analysis components, this becomes somewhat easier. Even without these machines (and of course they cannot be used in scoring essays), self-analysis must be considered.

Examine the students' tests. Was there a fact or concept that stands out as poorly answered by the entire class? If so, admit to yourself that you probably did not do a good job teaching it. If it is a concept critical to the development progression of your course content (i.e. - a basic theorem in math, a set of laws in science, or a sentence structure rule in English), then go back and re-teach if differently and re-test it separately. Do not fall into the pattern of "I teach; you learn" and blindly go through the course heedless of student errors. The students honestly will not think less of you, in fact they will appreciate your candor and concern for their academic welfare if you do re-teach missed material. If the problem is with singular students rather than an entire class, you may consider giving them the individual tests back for correcting with an open notebook or textbook. This places some degree of responsibility on them because it is not your failing that a few missed the concept when most of the class understood it.

Even if the missed fact or component is not something that will affect their lives, then the least you should do is make a note to avoid the faulty teaching next time around. I have found it necessary to jot down a pencil notation right on my lesson plans for the next time I teach that concept. Do not trust your memory to these things - they must be written down.

You may even wish to tape record your lectures so that you can evaluate them at a later date. This may not be practical, or even necessary, but it can help a new teacher who is experiencing difficulty.

Search for new techniques. If lecture produces
confusion, resort to handouts. Use notesheets in place
of the blackboard; try oral reports instead of a tedious
listing of people, places, or things. Have students
teach a particular idea; bring in guest speakers, even
colleagues who do a better job in that particular
area than you do.

One of the better ways to self-evaluate is to have
the students provide input as to a course's strengths or
weaknesses. The evaluation form need not be anything
ornate. Included is a sample copy of one that I have
used. Solicit candid input, examine it, improve on the
suggested weaknesses and dwell on the indicated
strengths.

STUDENT EVALUATION FORM: R. TRIMBLE

PLEASE ANSWER OBJECTIVELY AND HONESTLY.   NO SIGNATURE
REQUIRED.

1.   What was your overall opinion of the course & the
     instructor?

2.   If you were teaching this course, what would you do
     differently?   Cite what you felt was the course's
     weakpoint.

3.   What points were strongest about the course, the way
     it was presented?   Cite what aspects of the course
     you would like to see continued or expanded upon.

4.   What was your favorite segment of the material
     presented in the course (i.e. - your favorite
     unit (s))?

5.   What lecture (s) would you do or not do relevant to
     this course?

6.   What assignment (s) would you do or not do relevant
     to this course?

7.   Did you learn from this course?

8.   Comments:

OVER 100 IDEAS FOR YOUR CLASSROOM
AN ANNOTATED CHECKLIST

This portion of the book you may find most useful
around mid-year when you begin to ask yourself, what can
I do that is different? You want to liven up the class
and give them a change of pace, so you ask what
alternatives you have. This checklist may help you. I
would like to thank some of my colleagues, especially
Tony Trebino of Manasquan High School and John Verilla,
Jr. of Hawthorne High School, for their inter-
disciplinary assistance.

1. CHAPTER OUTLINING: This is generally considered
    more effective for students than the traditional
    underlining that we all do in our college texts.
    Underlining often supplants a careful reading of the
    text and certainly the re-writing involved in
    chapter outlining is a proven reinforcement tool.

2. TEXT UNDERLINING: Underlining is acceptable if the
    student owns the book of course, but read the
    cautionary words above.

3. MAPS: Students of all levels like maps. Plus, they
    are good drill devices. Furthermore, geography has
    been repeatedly cited as an area of need for
    improvement in education. When giving them to
    history classes, especially upper levels, try to
    include boundary changes such as the acquisition of
    territory United States or the Holy Roman Empire
    becoming modern Germany. Be sure to show students
    how to use map indeces. Surprisingly few students
    utilize them.

4. "YOU ARE THERE" ESSAYS: A good sense of creative
    writing can be instilled with these essays. Have
    the students put themselves in a particular time or
    place after you have created the scenario with your
    lectures or films. For example, teach a unit on
    slavery and then have the students write a diary
    page as if they were living in that time period and
    had involvement in the institution of slavery. This
    can be done in units for World War I and II, Fantasy
    Literature, Sci-Fi Literature, and so on.

5. TEXT QUESTIONS: Pick and choose the questions that
    pertain to your material. Do not just assign entire
    pages or end-of-chapter questions. Furthermore, if
    you utilize a text that does not contain such
    questions, you may wish to make up your own set as

you read the text yourself. I have found that even the top-level students need the sort of structured approach to a chapter that questions provided. Realize, however, that most students, when looking up assigned questions will not read the entire chapter. Thus complex and important chapters may still need outlining rather than question-answering.

6. READ-AND-ORALLY REPORT: When your class content is very current and magazine/newspaper articles abound, it can be a good practice to save the various articles that appear, pass them out to class members, and then have individual students orally report on their article. This will stimulate round-table discussion and will cover a multitude of articles more efficiently than having every student read every article.

7. ORAL REPORTS: These are a must for just about any class as they expose the student to public speaking. However, you may wish to take some of the pressure off by having the students circle their desks around the center of the room and have them present their data while still seated. It lightens the atmosphere. Ask for volunteers to begin each period. This way, if you have set aside only a certain number of days to allow oral reports, then the reluctant speaker cannot say that you did not give him time to present his work. Enforce attentiveness by telling the class that there will be a quiz on the orally-presented data. Many times students mentally dismiss information presented by anyone other than the teacher. It is a good idea to stress to the students that they should try to tie in some sort of audio-visual aid such as pictures, maps, diagrams, etc. It is imperative that you stress to the students that they may not directly read their reports. They will all do this unless you specifically state otherwise. Tell them to tie in dramatics, theatrics and enthusiasm.

8. FILMS, VIDEOS AND FILMSTRIPS: Use those that are directly relevant to your class and narrate them as they are presented. The in-class emphasis of significant points is a proven and successful tactic. I have tried study sheets with prepared film questions, but the narration method is best. Do not be afraid to stop the projector tp interject your points.

9. FILMSTRIPS WITH A STUDY QUESTIONNAIRE: Filmstrips can often be doze-off time unless they are made to be relevant. One way to make them so is to prepare a set of specific questions based on the film so the students will have to follow along attentively. Collect them at the end of the class. This also is useful for teaching freshmen or lower-level classes how to view filmstrips.

10. ORAL READINGS: There is no problem with assigning material to be read aloud in class, provided that you remember two points- a) do not embarrass the slow-reader; and b) keep the passages short.

11. CROSSWORD PUZZLES: Make your own. Start with a piece of graph paper and begin lining up words from your subject material. Interlace them as any crossword puzzle would have them. Darken in the spaces you do not use; number the beginning of each word in down or across sequences. Make up your key. Erase the initial words you wrote in and there you have it. Photocopy as needed.

12. WORDGRAMS: Make your own again. Use graph paper and interlace key words from your subject material in up, down, across, and diagonal fashion. Fill in the spaces with other various letters. Make up a key; photocopy as needed.

13. NEWSPAPER FRONT PAGES: Assign the students a particular time frame in a history lesson and have them draw up an imaginary front page to a newspaper of that time. Tell them you are looking for some degree of historical accuracy to the main story as well as a degree of imagination. Have them draw it up on oaktag or manila paper.

14. COLLEGE BOWL: A great way to review for a test or major exam, divide the class into teams. Since mine is a regional high school, I divide them up according to towns they live in. Fire review questions at them. They have fifteen seconds to answer and must answer through a spokesmen for the purpose of decorum. Keep score. The kids love it.

15. CLASS GAME - "CIVILIZATION": Teaching history, sociology, or humanities? I created a game painted on an old Ouiji board a few years back. It has fifteen lines across representing levels. The bottom ten lines are level A and the top five lines are level B. The student places a marker of

some sort at the bottom line and proceeds to work
his way up to the top of the board, thus reaching
"Civilization." He does this by drawing cards that
say things like "Metallurgy invented - jump two
spaces" or "Law codes devised - move two spaces," or
"Writing Develops - jump three spaces." Think of as
many trappings of civilization as you can. However,
add negative cards like, "Flood - drop two spaces"
or "Barbarians pillage land - drop three spaces."
The A and B levels enable only certain cards to
apply. For instance a society would have to
learn to write before it acquired an intelligentsia
or scholar class. Differentiate the more
sophisticated characteristics of society by
designating those cards (and make them few) "B level
only." Put the players in teams of two and set up
as many teams as you can on the board. Have one
student play while another records his moves, like a
diarist. The winner's diarist would then read the
record - this becomes a good learning tool on how a
society reaches civilization.

16. TWO - TEAM BLACKBOARD FOOTBALL: Divide the class
into two teams and fire questions that you would
classify in terms of yardage. Failure to get a
"first down" with easy, short-yardage questions
turns the round of questioning over the other team.
Furthermore, if a team cannot answer a question
and the other team gets it, this is a fumble or
interception. You can score touchdowns, field goals
and extra-points, based upon the difficulty of
questions and "field position." Use your
imagination.

17. BOOK REPORTS: My general rules for these types of
assignments are 1,000 words containing three areas
of focus. Students must summarize the work (show me
that they read the book and hit the author's main
message), critically analyze the work (what is
specifically good or bad about the book), and
discuss whether or not the book will help them in
their study in this class. I have found that
structure is a good practice when it comes to book
reports. Some students find it difficult to
distinguish between book reports and book reviews.
Basically, the difference as I see it lies in the
thrust of focus. If you want to emphasize summary
book content, then it is a book report. If you wish
to emphasize the interpretation of the writer's
message, his writing style, etc. then it is a book
review. My requirements hedge the bet between both

review and report. I like it that way. Also, do not hesitate to copy book reviews from newspapers on books dealing with your subject material. These can serve as guidelines of a sort.

18. MINI-REPORTS: I like to assign thousand word research reports on topics of direct focus. This helps marginal students in the techniques of paper writing. To assign these students full research/ thesis papers is asking too much. You may wish to decide as to requiring footnotes and bibliography. I do, as this is part of the learning process. Be sure to have the students narrow their topics down. I tell them that the longer the topic title, the more narrow the focus.

19. TERM PAPERS: This is the big one. I call for ten typed pages with footnotes and bibliography. I do not ask for a thesis, however I do ask the student to interpret and analyze data. Bear in mind that you must be aware of the academic level of your students in choosing to assign this type of paper or the type indicated in the preceding item.

20. DEBATES: This is a good marking period project. Have the students choose topics on their own, but on approval by you. Divide the class into three or four debates. Generally three-to-five students per side in a single debate is optimal. Once they arrive at the topic, divide them into the pro-side and the con-side and have each team choose a spokesman whose job it will be to direct the focus of his team's research and argument. You must meet with each group and offer the students specific arguments so that each debater is not saying the same thing. You must, therefore, set aside perhaps one class period per week for a month in order to hold in-class meeting times. Encourage the use of polls, charts, etc. for students to facilitate their side of the debate argument. By way of structure in the debate itself, I offer the following format:

DEBATES & DEBATE TOPICS

Dates:

Your group consists of the following members:

Suggested topics: gun control, raise N.J. drinking
age to 21, increase defense
budget, capital punishment, ERA
amendment, other topics of
agreed-upon nature.

Format: 1. Mr. Trimble will moderate.
2. Each side of debate (3 members) will
have 10 minutes to make its point - 3
minutes per speaker; there will be no
rebuttals or questions at this time.
3. Rebuttals - no single speaker will be
allowed more than 3 minutes; flow of
points/counter-point discussion will be
controlled.
4. Last 10-15 minutes of class will be
open to questions from general
classroom.
5. Class votes to see who wins the debate.

21. DIORAMA PROJECTS: Students in history classes might
enjoy making paper mache' battlefields, covered in
clay and then depicted with demolished plastic
buildings, HO-scale toy soldiers, lichen, sticklogs,
and whatever else the imagination can draw upon.
Similarly, students in English classes can set
scenes; students in science classes can re-create
famous experiments, and so on.

22. POLITICAL CARTOONS: Students in history, English,
political science and social issues classes can draw
their own political cartoons. One need not be a
great artist - just show the students how to label
drawn items properly. A good way to prepare this
lesson is to copy newspaper political cartoons onto
an overhead transparency by means of a Thermo-fax
machine. Show them on the classroom screen and have
the kids decipher them.

23. INDIVIDUALIZED PROJECTS: A good idea for a unit-
project and at the same time, appeal to the
individualized interests of each student, is to
assign their choice of supplemental learning
assignment. Pass out, or otherwise go over, ideas

such as artwork, scrapbooks, sketches, stitchery, mobiles, battle dioramas, short stories, oral reports, show-n-tells, and so forth dealing with an overall subject like World War II, Japanese history, or environmental science.

24. EDITORIAL WRITING: After covering a unit dealing with a controversial subject like nuclear energy, FDR's New Deal, or the Vietnam War, ask the students to write an editorial expressing their views. Tell them that editorials are succinct, to the point, and specific in nature. This assignment should be the coin-of-the-realm in journalism and social problems classes.

25. LABORATORY WORK: The old standby in science classes, this can be applied in computer classes and even upper-level history classes for the analysis of statistical data, etc.

26. TAPE-AND-RESPONSE: Particularly useful in foreign language classes, taped questions can be responded to aloud by the class or prepared as a supplemental assignment for the student having a problem and in need of further drill work. As a footnote, I have had the problem of having to miss an afternoon class due to a coaching commitment. When this happens often enough that the class suffers, I try to tape the lecture given in a previous class and then have the covering teacher simply play back the tape with the afternoon students taking notes as usual. Have them jot down questions in their notes as they might arise. It works better than you might think.

27. SURVEYS: An easy, but interesting, assignment is to give a sociology, history, or current issues class a survey/poll to do on a key social or current issue. The educational aspect however, is with the analysis, so spend time on that.

28. CORRECT THE ERRORS AS A CLASS: Take some student essays or math problems and have them copied on to overhead transparencies. Flash them on the board, minus the student's name, of course. It is good exercise to have the students correct their own errors - with discussion comes learning.

29. STUDENT-TEACHERS: Do you teach honors courses? Eighth grade? Why not have them tutor lower-level or problem students or perhaps even teach certain classes? Be careful, however. I have done this and

since the students are not usually gifted speakers
(skills are not as sharp), the idea here sounds
better than it actually is in practice. A good way
for prospective teachers to learn their trade might
be to video-tape their own lectures and then
critique them in class.

30. COMMUNITY PROJECTS: Depending upon the type of
class, you might consider volunteering your students
as a manpower pool. In art classes, I have seen
students involved with sign painting for the
community; environmental studies classes have
worked on duck feeding programs, recycling drives,
and stream-walking projects. Our geometry classes
coordinated with our environmental studies classes
on a mapping project that once saved a local borough
up to eight thousand dollars. Grant-projects like
oral interviews in history classes, energy saving
displays for science classes and so on can not only
serve the community, but also put a feather in your
cap and give your school some positive publicity.
One of the first steps in such an endeavor is to
make it known to community civic groups, via
personal contact or letters, that you are interested
in having your classes involved and that the group
being contacted may call on your people for
assistance in their projects. Many times both hands
will wash each other here. One cautionary note -
make sure that the students are working for a grade.
If not, their failure to show up for a commitment on
your part can be embarrassing.

31. MODEL UNITED NATIONS: Assign each student to a
specific nation, have them research that country's
political, social, economic, and resource picture,
and then structure your UN sessions complete with
table arrangement, Secretary-General, signs denoting
each nation and representative, and podium. Present
one key issue for debate and instruct the students
that they should debate, caucus, vote, and think
along the lines and interests of the country they
represent. Speech classes can benefit from such a
project, too. Perhaps an inter-disciplinary
approach might be useful.

32. ROLE-PLAYING: This is particularly useful in
classes such as psychology and family living,
wherever inter-personal human relationships are
involved. Students can act out Freudian ego defense
mechanisms, family crisis intervention models, and
even the more elaborate project of hypothetical

marriages. In the latter, arrange for two students
to marry, have children and then have them manage
budgets and deal with crises as you pass them out on
3x5" cards: Joe loses his job, Mary is infertile,
Sue and Jim get a divorce.

33. NEWSPAPER CLIPPING FILE: When teaching current
events, social problems and classes of topical
content, have the students keep a news-clipping file
where they cut out newspaper articles that deal with
topics relevant to their class. Have them paste the
articles into a notebook along with summaries. Keep
the articles dated so that you can trace the
student's work over the entire marking period, not
just the last week before the grades were closed
out.

34. MOCK TRIAL: A colleague used to make this the focal
point of his law classes. He chose judge, jury,
witnesses, attorneys, stenographers, police chief
and anyone else germane to the project. He then
passed out a crime scenario (this must be very
carefully developed), gave the class a week to
develop their cases and then went to trial. The
outcome was determined by the jury. Another type of
mock trial is a a simple example employed during a
lecture on perhaps witch-craft, the French
Revolution, Spanish Inquisition, or even Stalin's
Show Trials. Select three students and ask them to
leave the room. Prep your "inquisitors" by having
them ask the accused (those outside the room) to
recite the Pledge of Allegiance or the Lord's Prayer
and/or sing the National Anthem or "Onward Christian
Soldiers." You'll find them guilty, rest assured.
This illustrates the misuse of justice during these
times. It takes only five minutes.

35. SIMULATED ARCHAEOLOGY SITE: An intriguing project
for anthropology or ancient history classes is to
obtain a section of school property, perhaps ten
feet by ten feet, open it up, bury projects made by
students in class, and then have them excavate the
site systematically as if it were a genuine
archaeological site and they were actual
archaeologists. After instructing the class on the
techniques of excavating, cataloging, and recording
data, select four grid captains and divide the site
into quadrants. After this, the excavation will
guide itself. All you do is quietly oversee. I
have had "sophisticated" juniors and seniors in high
school play-act in these glorified Easter Egg Hunts

successfully for years. It is easy after the first dig - merely bury the unearthed artifacts in the open hole, cover it up and let next semester's class dig it all up again.

36. MOCK PRESIDENTIAL CAMPAIGN: This one worked beautifully! Choose jobs for all students involved, preferably an entire grade-class (i.e. - the junior class). Jobs would include candidates (two or three), media advisors to print posters and take photos, speech writers, state and local campaign chairmen, co-workers, and so on. Then have each candidate and staff work to get their man elected on a set Election Day. Have them give speeches, put up posters, issue press releases to be read in classes. You may wish to have the candidates views correspond with actual candidates in a real election year or you may wish to choose your own fictitious people. Make it a national election scenario. The finale before the voting could be a school assembly depicting a simulated political convention. Present the party platform, nominate the candidates, have them make their final speeches and then vote. I did this in my second year of teaching and it is one my fonder memories.

37. QUOTATION IDENTIFICATION SHEET: Put a quotation or series of quotations on a ditto sheet and have the students identify who said it, why it was said, when it was said and what it means. This can be used in most humanities electives, English classes, poetry classes and history classes. Use actual quotations and stress that the student's reasoning is more important than their correct answer.

38. GUEST SPEAKERS: Be careful here. Guest speakers are not often teachers and therefore may be unaccustomed to speaking before school classes; similarly, not every class can handle or appreciate an outside speaker. It can be embarrassing to have a person invited in only to be eaten alive by a class who cares little about the topic. Prep the class about the topic and about what you expect in terms of behavior. Threaten them. Take notes and quiz the class when through. Have questions ready so that if the time drags, you can fill the breach. It is always good courtesy to send a written thank you note after the speaker departs.

39. STUDENT SPEAKERS: Why not have some of your better students speak before Brownie troops, elementary grades, and so on? If your subject is science, environmental studies, archaeology, Indian lore, and so on, outside grade-school groups readily look for such speakers and presentations. Have the student-speakers prepare hands-on-demonstrations however, as this best appeals to the younger crowd. Leave them with a vocabulary list or wordgram to reinforce the lesson.

40. STUDENT MANPOWER: It has long intrigued me as to the extent and possibilities of utilizing students as a manpower resource. Shop classes can literally build buildings and what a great sense of accomplishment and pride in school and self will be garnered form such a contribution! I have seen school industrial arts classes build non-foundational homes and actually sell them through their accounting and advertising classes. In addition to this idea, I have already discussed the concept of student/community projects, but I am here referring to students working for their school. Have them paint walls, build lockers in metal shop classes, build weight training equipment for the gym and so on.

41. READING PASSAGES ALOUD TO CLASS: I have referred to this earlier but it is worthwhile to enhance a lecture with some outside reading. It tends to bring your lecture to life. Furthermore psychologists and learning specialists tell us that it transmits the joy of reading to the students. Just do not over-use this technique as it can be boring if the readings ramble on and are not pertinant. Be selective in the passages you choose to recite. The more vivid, lurid, and sanguine, the better.

42. AMNESTY DAY: If you have a class that is not especially motivated when it comes to homework, why not motivate them with an un-announced day of working on homework during class time - and they will not receive the late penalty points! The kids jump on it and you will be surprised as to how many homework assignments come in... which probably would not have come in otherwise. This is most effective toward the end of a marking period when the kids have piled up missed homeworks and begun to ask the age-old, "What can I do to pass?"

43. ESSAY CONTEST: Why not run a contest for the best
    editorial, short story, descriptive essay, or
    whatever? Offer a certificate for a prize or put
    out five bucks from your own pocket. Do you know any
    merchants in town? Maybe they will put up a gift
    certificate as a prize. You can be the sole judge
    or have a panel of teachers. Furthermore, give the
    winning essay(s) to the teacher who coordinates the
    fine arts magazine or school newspaper. Some local
    papers might even publish the work.

44. SLIDES AND PHOTOGRAPHY: When you go on a field
    trip, take pictures and have slides made up. It has
    been my experience that you are not able to take the
    same trip year after year. With slides, you can
    preserve the trip and have more students benefit
    from it. Suggest the idea to a pupil who might be
    going on a family trip to a location that deals with
    your course content. Slides cost less than pictures
    and can be better utilized in class. Assign a
    student camera-buff a project wherein he photographs
    relevent data such as beach erosion, historic sites,
    tree types, pollution, etc.

45. CLASS MUSEUM: Take a table, window sill, or set
    aside a section of your room for a class museum. I
    have seen archaeological artificts shown, private
    interest collections displayed, models of airplanes
    from the World Wars, dioramas of soldiers in battle,
    and hands-on physics experiments. Realize that there
    is a danger of theft or vandalism, so take
    precautionary measures.

46. MUSIC AS A REFLECTIONS OF HISTORY: If you teach
    history or music, a valuable lesson can be in the
    form of music selections that reflect the moods of
    countries during their periods of history. Take the
    rebellious rock music from the 1960's as an example
    of anti-war sentiment against the conflict in
    Vietnam. Play Russian classical music to reflect
    the anger and discontent of pre-revolutionary
    Russia.

47. POETRY AS A REFLECTION OF HISTORY: Similar to the
    above, poetry can be used to reflect a country's
    mood and history. Selections from Pushkin, Kipling
    and others can be valuable.

48. INTERVIEW ASSIGNMENTS: Have history students
    interview people who fought in World War II, Korea
    or Vietnam; have sociology students trace social

change with their grandparents. The interviews may be taped and placed on file in the library if they are particularly noteworthy, or they may simply be written on prepared interview guidelines-sheets. Aside from the actual intent or focus of the lesson, the value of this type of assignment will be an enhancement of older people, their image and their worth in the eyes of students.

49. CURRENT EVENTS BULLETIN BOARDS: Key articles about newsworthy items and current events can be displayed for student interest. A tried and true lesson, it can be effective.

50. TERM SHEETS AND VOCABULARY LISTS: Another age-old assignment, but a must for history, science, foreign language, certain social studies and certain English classes.

51. THEOREM SHEETS: Math teachers who do not deal in vocabulary terms, but do work with theorems, can vividly reinforce key theorems with theorem review sheets.

52. ORAL PRESENTATION OF PAPERS AND REPORTS: In having students orally present their papers and reports to the class, your motivation can be four-fold. You want your students exposed to oral reporting, you want to truly determine if a student did a report on his own or copied it, you feel that an additional passing grade (which such an oral report will most probably be) will help a borderline class. Furthermore, by orally presenting papers, the entire class can benefit from an area of what would otherwise be individual research. Oral presentation of papers and book reports is considered a solid practice in honors classes, not to mention some college classes.

53. PROBLEM ASSIGNMENTS: If you teach college-type courses to students of a better-than-average academic standing and/or if you have a textbook that lacks supplemental questions, you may wish to list specific essays of a directed research nature. Make them broad, sweeping and analytical in nature. These are not to be single-sentence text questions, but rather those which require more thought and preparation. These may be designed to reinforce work you cover in class lectures or they may be designed to give the students exposure to areas of study or points of view that you will not have time

to cover. It is a good exercise in directed research.

54. IDENTIFICATION SHEET ON FAMOUS PEOPLE: Write up a list of three or four-line descriptions beginning with "I am...." and then close with "Who am I?" This is good drill work for a younger history class.

55. CURRENT EVENTS: Although I have never been completely satisfied with this technique, I have covered current events by having the students cut relevant news-clippings from the paper or news-magazine they receive at home. Have them summarize the article's contents or it might not have been read. These may be submitted singly or compiled as part of the news-clipping file suggested earlier. This is done after you have gone over the major current event issues in class. Having students submit the articles first simply does not work for me. The students lack the background data; understanding suffers.

56. TIMELINES: There are several approaches here, but two that work well are to simply assign all events you may have emphasized in a given history unit to be placed on a home-made timeline. Or you can provide the timeline on a ditto with the key events numbered and have the students place the numbers along the timeline. This type of assignment is especially important in a history unit where you have covered several wide-ranging and somewhat unrelated issues and events.

57. TEST OR QUIZ CORRECTION IN CLASS: If, and only if, the question content in a particular quiz or test is completely objective (i.e. - containing black- and-white, right-or-wrong answers), you may wish to have the students exchange papers for oral grading done in class. It gives immediate feedback and thus, reinforcement. It saves a little time correcting the work, too.

58. MATH DRILL SHEETS: Another old standby from the math teachers. Write up problem sheets for class or homework. The essential point, however, is that the students show their work, not just the answers. This helps you, the teacher, see where errors are made and furthermore, helps minimize copying among students.

59. VIDEOS: Local library and audio-visual associations and stores will offer videos, just as they did when 16mm films used to be available. However, do not limit yourself to these. When a good educational television show comes on, tape your own. If you do not like it, you can later erase it, but taping a T.V. show and using it in class can enable more students to see it and in a better educational environment. Generally, taping for non-profit, classroom use does not infringe on copyright laws.

60. COMPUTER SOFTWARE GAMES: These are new, varied and constantly being created by computer companies. The best idea is to order catalogs from the computer companies and keep abreast of the latest games. I am not referring to the simple "gallery-shoot" games. Moreover, the use of computers is a new, emerging field which teachers and students will have to become familiar with. Games include such concepts as statistical analysis of historical events and trends, economic management, scientific programs, word processing for English classes, and map work for geography classes. Since so many schools today have computer labs, it is worthwhile to look into these usages of the computers for the sake of the total education for your students and for your classroom diversity.

61. MILITARY SIMULATION GAMES: I once had a class of military history buffs that comprised the bulk of a Modern European History class. I devoted one week to playing military simulation games, such as those put out by Avalon-Hill. These games provide the battlefield terrain and logistics and then leave it to you to re-fight the battle. You may wish to utilize the same tactics as the generals did in the actual event or avoid their mistakes. These games abound - the Franco-Prussian War, Spartans, War at Sea (W.W.II), Air War Over Europe, and so on. What is educationally advantageous is to have the students write a short report at the conclusion of their battle comparing what happened in their conflict with what happened historically. I advise this for only upper-level and highly motivated classes.

62. CHILD OBSERVATIONS: This is an excellent project for psychology, child development, or family life classes. It should be a major paper. Have the students select a child (relative, neighbor, friend) of pre-adolescent age and, with the permission of the parent or guardian, observe the child in formal settings. The students must be taught what to look for. Consider the play activity, school and other structured settings, relationships with siblings, friends and adults, and their performance in a battery of informal tests such as drawing themselves and their family, motor activities, word and puzzle games, and so on. This is generally a well-accepted project.

63. TEST REVIEW SHEETS: If you hate to review, as I do, test review sheets can help. If you are passing these out to the students put them on colored paper or half-sheets so that if your review sheets look like the test copies, the students cannot write them out at home, slip them into the classroom and submit them as the test work. Provide the students with the general subject areas of the questions for the exam. These should not be direct answers, of course, but rather a generalized topical suggestion. For instance, if a question reads: "Match the Romantic Era authors with their most significant works," have the study sheet tell the students to know Romantic Era authors and works. You have not given them any answers, but rather directed their study. This is an acceptable practice. Tell them of dates to know, element numbers, names, and so on. As for essays, I list some half-dozen and tell them that I will select their exam essays from the listing provided. I select two or three from the list.

64. MILITARY STRATEGY LESSON: An interesting way to teach a battle lesson is to project a map of the battle region on a blackboard with the overhead projector. Give the students their logistical data and then have them plan out the battle. I have done this with the Union strategies against the South in the Civil War and with the grand strategy for defeating the Axis Powers in Europe in World War II. By flashing the map on the blackboard, you can draw on it with chalk.

65. PRE-TESTS & POST-TESTS: Many districts mandate that these sort of tests be administered. Simply put, a pre-test is given prior to a unit or course being taught. A hint for the teacher is to tell the kids to answer only those questions that they are absolutely positive as to the correctness of their answer. This eliminates a guessing score, or "Monkey Score" wherein anyone can generally score up to ten percent correct. A post-test is often the final exam. The comparison is then made between how many students knew the course or unit material prior to your teaching it and then how many know the material after you teach it. If you work the pre-test right, invariably you look good on these. If you are going to be held accountable on students passing the final exam, then you may be forced to teach to it, review for it, and prep your students with study guides. It is a shame that education sometimes comes down to that, but when it does, you must decide on your reaction.

66. FOREIGN LANGUAGE LISTENING COMPREHENSION: For teachers of foreign languages, the taped, oral listening test is a must. It is simply a series of taped statements which the students either translate or respond to. It is a fundamental, sound drill.

67. TAPED CARTOONS AND PROGRAMS FOR FOREIGN LANGUAGES: I have seen foreign language teachers, especially Spanish teachers, tape television shows that are broadcast in Spanish (cartoons are a hit with younger students), and then play the show for their classes. They may ask their students to respond in writing or simply watch and translate mentally.

68. GRAPHS: Students must be exposed to analytical thinking via graphs and charts. Do not pass off this job to math teachers alone. Geography, history, science and sociology teachers can make use of graphs and should do so. A good technique is to make a copy to flash on the overhead projector, show it on the screen and then have the students analyze as a class. You may wish to conclude the lesson with the viewing of another graph-types: pie graphs, bar graphs, line graphs, etc. -- and have each student turn in a written analysis on his own. This tests their

understanding. All too often, students gloss
over graphs in their textbooks without bothering to
really examine and analyze them.

69. CLASS GAME - FINANCES, TAXES & MONEY: Begin by
making a batch of paper money. It need not be
complex; make up copies on a ditto master and run
off plenty. If you are teaching subjects like
taxes, family planning, French Revolution taxation,
U.S. History Stock Market Crash, U.S. History
Gold- Silver Controversy in the 1890's, and so on,
distribute the money, place the class in a tax-
paying scenario that you create to suit your needs,
and then control the amount of tax collected by
student-collectors. It makes for a great futuristic
experience; since we cannot expose them to death, at
least we can prepare them for taxes.

70. CLASS GAME - LIBERAL-CONSERVATIVE: A good way to
expose students to politically divergent views as
well as test the political leanings of your audience
is to play this game. Pass out sheets of scrap
paper and have the kids number from 1-10. You will
then read out Issue One (example - Military
Spending). Play a bit of the ham actor here as you
will then present an ultra-liberal point of view
that should be given a value weight of 10. (Example
- "We should totally scrap all military spending and
disarm...I'm sure that the Russians will follow
suit!"). Then read the students an equally ultra-
conservative position which would carry a weight of
1. (Example - Make it a law the EVERYONE serves
four years in the military, carries weapons, and
spends 50 percent of the government's money on the
military budget...). Now, most students would not
agree with either extreme position, but they will
probably lean toward either 1 or 10. Those who
favor the liberal, or 10, side should put a 6, 7, 8
or 9 on their paper depending upon how closely they
ally themselves with the extremist position taken by
you. Numbers 2, 3, 4, and 5 represent those on the
conservative stance. Present ten key social
political issues in this manner. Have fun acting
them out with the extreme red-neck and wide-eye
liberal postures. After the kids have selected their
numerical sentiments on the 1 - 10 scale for each
issue, have them total the numbers and divide by

ten. On the blackboard, draw up a line graph such as
this:

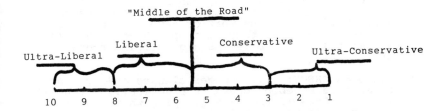

"Middle of the Road"

Liberal   Conservative

Ultra-Liberal   Ultra-Conservative

10   9   8   7   6   5   4   3   2   1

Have the students plot the lowest number they put
down and then the highest. Draw an oval connecting
the two numbers and this will reflect their
narrow-or-broad mindedness. Then have them plot
the average. Although your interpretation may dif-
fer, I like to view the range of liberal, conservative, or middle-of-the road within the scope shown
above.

71. TRIVIA: Why not play History Trivia with questions
specifically geared to your course of study? Or you
can take questions right from the box of some of the
more popular trivia games marketed today, selecting
those questions that deal with history, literature,
science, etc. I have seen foreign language trivia
played, too. You may wish to put the students into
teams that may foster a competitive atmosphere. You
may even wish to use exam questions; this becomes a
great way to review.

72. "WHAT IF" ESSAYS: If you are looking for a change
of pace assignment that also involves higher
cognitive thinking skills, why not assign either a
short essay or longer term research paper dealing
with what may have happened if the South had won
the Civil War, or if Hitler had not been elected, or
if Stalin had been purged in 1924?

73. MATCH GAME: When you teach a unit with a host of
names, authors, scientific terms, battles, etc.,
you might try having the students make up their own
match games. One column will, of course, have the
name of the item while the second lists, in
scrambled sequence, an identifying explanation.

They will match the item to its identification. You have done this for tests, so why not have the students make up their own? You should provide the subject listing. You can even have the best student - made match games re-produced on a ditto master for distribution as class work or have the entire class exchange the games they made up. Having the kids answer the games serves as a good reinforcement drill.

74. NOTEBOOK CHECK: For younger classes and for poorer classes, a notebook check is practically essential. You must know if they are grasping what you are trying to convey in a lecture. Check their notebooks during a test or class exercise. Assign it as a grade, as this gives the entire project more credibility and rewards those students who take notes diligently. The notebook should contain all handouts; the notes should be organized and relatively neat. For grading purposes, list on a ditto the topics you will be looking for in their notes. Check off each item as it appears in their books. Correct their note-taking errors as this enhances the teaching of student study skills. Do not make this a surprise grade - tell them at the onset of the course so that the marginal students at least make some effort to take notes and keep dittos. Place a mark on the notebooks you check to avoid their being passed around the class from gamesman to gamesman.

75. NUTRITION DAY: For science or foreign language classes, you may wish to have the students prepare foods relevant to the major food groups or to the cultural cuisine served in the countries of the language studied.

76. COLLAGES: For groups of lower ability, have them cut out pictures of a thematic nature and paste them onto poster boards for collages. Themes could be of a wide variety -- safety, alcoholism, food and nutrition, current events, health, sports, history and so on.

77. CLASS GAME: ORIGINS OF WORLD WAR I: To show the secret alliance system and its impact on the beginnings of World War I, pass out 3 x 5" cards with the names of the principle nations of the time shown on them. Next, pass out cards to other

students with the names of the lesser states, colonial territories, and power vacuum regions on them. On the latter cards, write in "secretly allied with _____." Now have any two of the little client states declare war and bring the two combatant students to the front of the room. Indicate to the class how this conflict should be localized and insignificant, but watch how it escalates. Ask anyone who has a card showing an alliance, major or minor, with either of the two belligerents to join them in the front of the room. You will see that virtually every nation/student will come forward on one side or the other. This is a short, illustrative exercise that only takes up a matter of minutes from a lecture. It serves to punctuate the presentation. You should reinforce it by showing the danger of having super-powers ally themselves with small, radical states.

78. HANGMAN: The old game of hangman can be modified into a learning exercise by using words related to your course of study. Play it right on the blackboard.

79. PRO-CON ESSAYS: You can pick out two articles that pose divergent viewpoints on the same issue. After teaching material relevant to the topic, have the students read the words of the writers, consider your class notes, and then pose their own view in a pro-con editorial essay. I have used this specifically in topics such as abortion, gun control, nuclear power for commercial use, nuclear arms proliferation, and so on.

80. COUNTER-ARGUMENT ESSAYS: I teach Environmental Studies within my varied class load. Call it coaching, but I pass out a ditto with eight superficial, emotionally charged statements by a hypothetical non-environmentalist on it. Simple sayings like, "Why should we bother to save wetlands? They're just wastelands except for a few birds and clams..." Have the students write out responses. Demand specificity, statistics (that you have provided them with during the course of the class lecture), and brevity. This type of essay as well as that indicated above in item 79 are good exercises in critical thinking.

81. OPTION ASSIGNMENTS: At one point the educational
    vogue was "individualization." Although the concept
    had its merits, it proved a bit unworkable because
    of its lack of structure. One valuable lesson from
    individualized learning, however, can be to appeal
    to the students' select interests, hobbies and
    talents. When assigning a project, give them a
    ditto listing a variety of project-types geared to
    the same unit. Instead of assigning written reports
    to all students, give them an option of maps, oral
    reports, artwork, short stories, and so on. I
    suggest that you weight each according to a grade as
    I have found that the kids pick the easiest
    assignment of the batch if they are all equal in
    grade-weight. Perhaps one project would get them a
    C while another one gets them an A.

82. MEDIA PROJECT: Does you school have a radio or
    cable television station? Granted, few do, but at
    the very least your school does have a newspaper.
    (If one does not exist, then start one!).
    Utilization of media resources can be a worthwhile
    project. Produce your own public awareness
    campaigns or documentaries, film travel-logs, radio
    interviews, and so on. My Environmental Studies
    classes once ran a regular newspaper column entitled
    "Eco-logically Speaking." It was a great learning
    experience to have students prepare and write this
    piece and then have it published. I have seen Media
    classes produce films; science classes can produce
    documentaries for grade-school use. Art classes can
    produce plays, both televised and for radio, as well
    as copies of work from the "Artist of the Month" in
    the school newspaper. Some schools have in-school
    cable network hook-ups. If so, why not produce a
    weekly newsbroadcast of school events?

83. MEET THE PRESS: This is essentially a socio-drama.
    Students would be paired into teams for the purposes
    of research and interviewing. One student would
    play the interviewer, the other the subject. The
    subject would be a person of either historical or
    current event notoriety. In front of the class,
    the interview would be conducted and the students
    would be graded on the use of in-depth materials,
    clarity and organization of presentation, and
    portrayal of the subject's attitudes and thoughts.
    Along the same lines, you can have a student(s)

present the weekly current events update just as if he were a newscaster on television. Rotate the assignment around the room.

84. MINI-BIOGRAPHIES: If you have a unit with a great many names to remember (i.e. - the Greek Golden Age, the Romantic writers, classical musicians, contributors to the 18th-19th century Age of Science), then it can be worthwhile to have the students prepare short biographical data sketches. These can be presented orally in brief, round-table presentations or they can be typed on to ditto masters handed out and then run off by you after having been written out by the students. A quiz is usually a good follow-up to ensure the reading of the material or attentiveness to the talks; a match-game quiz is perhaps easiest to grade. Type up a ditto with the name to be reported on and just enough space for a line or two of notes. You can assign the names off this sheet and the students can take their notes off it, too, as the reports are presented.

85. MAIN IDEAS DRILL: Given younger classes and classes of lower academic ability, you may wish to help them discern the author's main ideas in a written piece. Run off newspaper articles, essays, source readings, or whatever. Have the students look for the five main points made by the author. Or have them write what they see as the single essential point made by the writer. The student responses should be written, too. This drill not only helps students look for the main points to remember but it also helps the teacher spot student deficiencies in this area.

86. TIME CAPSULE: This idea has always intrigued me. Why not take an anthropology, sociology, or history class and have them select materials to be buried in a weather-proof time capsule on school property? Materials selected could come from newspapers, taped news broadcast, current items of memorabilia, essays, photos, listings of current world events and issues, and then noteworthy pieces of information relevant to the students themselves, their school, and their class. All contributors should be mentioned by name. If you teach elementary school, have them bury their time capsule in fourth grade and then unearth it as eighth graders; if high school, go from freshmen to

senior year or simply place a five or ten year
lifespan on it, making a new capsule every year. Be
sure to include class pictures as these make for a
good laugh. Of course, the longer the time capsule
can remain in the "vault," then the more valuable it
becomes.

87. BRAINSTORMING: This is an often mis-used term. It
requires a special technique or it does not work.
In brainstorming, the teacher is merely a secretary
recording ideas; you are, of course, a mentor in the
sense that you will have to correct factual errors,
but the key is not to evaluate ideas. Accept any
and all thoughts. Start with a problem or premise
and have the students work out ideas as to causality
or solutions. Problem: world terrorism. Come up
with as many solution concepts as the class can
muster. Allow no dissent, disdain, or derogatory
and evaluative comments from fellow students. Accept
all ideas, outlandish or as logical as they might
be. You may not contribute. As another example,
have the students come up with as many causes for
the Russian Revolution of 1917 as they can. I once
had a Russian History class work up some forty
causes. I had a United States History class of
sophomores come up with thirty-two causes for the
American Civil War. This is an intriguing exercise
and one that really opens up a class. If you have a
class that is truly reticent, you may wish to have
them anonymously write down at least three solutions
to the to the problem to be discussed. Once you
gather all of your ideas through the brainstorming
method, write down all of them on the blackboard and
as a class, go over each one, re-writing, refining,
omitting, and re-phrasing to hammer out your final
solution.

88. FACT-SHEETS: Preparation and distribution of fact-
sheets can be interesting and eye-opening. When
teaching units on energy, scientific problems,
environmental issues, or social problems, have the
students research these topics to come up with as
many random statistics related to the issue as can
be found. For instance, my Environmental Studies
classes are always introduced to a new unit with a
fact sheet; it defines the problem and vividly shows
the students that a problem does exist. Recycling:
Americans throw out 80 billion bottles and cans
every year -- more than the entire continent of

Africa produces and enough to encircle the globe over 300 times if they were placed end-to-end. A sheet of statistics such as these will boggle the mind. As a community project, present them in a flyer or handbill. We did this when trying to get the town to put up a recycling center. Just make sure your facts are pertinant as well as accurate.

89. PANEL REPORTS AND FORUMS: A good way to present information to the class is from the class. Instead of having individualized oral reporting, why not put the students together in a panel of three. All three could take some aspect of the oral presenta-tion or they could split responsibilities into research-art-oral wherein one writes the report, one provides maps or artwork (audio-visual effects), and the other serves as the commentator. If you have students who might be handicapped in some intellectual capacity and have been main-streamed into your classroom or if you have students who simply, for one reason or another, cannot do oral reports, the this method is a good way to get them credit, have them contribute, and avoid the confrontation or problems of their not doing an oral report. It is a good idea to allow for question-answer during this time as it truly tests the panel's knowledge of their topic and does involve the class in what can be an active interchange.

90. POSITION PAPER: My classes have done two of these over the years. One dealt with the 1980 Iranian hostage crisis and the other with nuclear-freeze and disarmament. I offer these topics only as illustrative examples. Take a controversial and current issue, one that often has many divergent opinions as to a solution. Allow the class to brainstorm for as many solutions as possible (Refer to the brainstorming techniques mentioned in item 87.) Fill the blackboard. Accept any and all ideas, no mater how radical. Allow for no criticism at this point. Then go back to each item, discussing, re-phrasing, and voting as to whether or not it should be included in the position paper. The majority rules. Remember that it is the students' project, so do not serve as a censor, but you can and should correct factual errors and present ideas that may modify the concept toward positive ends. Once you have whittled down the solutions, have the class vote on order of

presentation of the listed solutions and have them
compose an introductory sentence for your position
paper. Assign a student to type it. Read the rough
copy to the class for any late additions or
deletions; re-type, and then have the students sign
it -- optional, of course. Make copies and send
them to the newspapers, local official and
congressmen. Then wait for the response.

91. SOCRATIC METHOD: Plato once said that his mentor,
the great Socrates, used to drive people to
frustration by never answering a question and only
posing further ones. Try a lesson in this fashion.
Set up a skeleton concept of prepared questions
once you have assigned the students outside work in
the topical area. The latter idea is important --
the students must have the background. Then fire
question after question at them, allowing the
discussion to flow the way it will. Remember,
answer none. If a student asks you a question,
throw it back out to the students and let them
answer it. This is not a good way to present
factual material, but it is an excellent way to
reinforce learned material. I assign a chapter
outline on the Industrial Revolution to my Honors
and Modern European History students and then hit
them with who, why, where, when, what and why not.
Assign a series of articles to read or have the
class watch a movie to provide the background
data.

92. CHART WORKSHEETS: It is of course good to expose
students to abstract thinking and one of the ways
to accomplish this is with the use of charts that
they fill in, compose, or otherwise work on either
in class or for homework. Make your own charts; you
need not buy them. I have made up charts dealing
with the social, economic, religious and political
composition of the thirteen colonies, the
accomplishments of the various Chinese dynasties,
the powers of the various branches of the U.S.
government, and comparative factors in the four
great political revolutions in modern western
history. I can envision science charts, geography
charts, health charts, physical education charts,
and so on. Simply employ charts as another way to
reinforce concepts learned in class.

93. STATISTICAL ANALYSIS: Pass out statistical data
sheets that you have photocopied from books and then
have the students analyze them. I have seen this
type of lesson used in regard to the shift of
Europe's Jewish population from 1935 to the present
day. Have the students look at gains and losses and
try to explain why they occurred. I have seen such
lessons used in classes dealing with population and
demography, the growth of urban centers during the
Industrial Revolution, and so on. Remember that many
types of college evaluative tests such as the
Advanced Placement Tests utilize statistical
analysis, so it behooves us to at least touch upon
such practices in our classes. This is another good
example of abstract thinking skills.

94. PREHISTORIC TECHNOLOGY: If you are teaching
Physical Anthropology or a unit on the American
Indian or early man, consider this. You can have
the students flake projectile points just as early
man did. Whereas early man used flint or argilite
and a bone or antler as a tool, you can accomplish
the same task with a small (about 1/2 x 1/2 inch)
rectangle of glass and a screwdriver. Have the
students wear goggles; you can probably borrow these
from the science or shop department. Include gloves.
Simply put, the technique calls for the student to
grasp the screwdriver close to the tip and, with
pressure, flake off chips of glass by pressing
toward the palm of that hand (see figure one).
There are eight edges to be cut, so have the
students perform this operation on all eight edges.
The rectangle of glass may, when the edge flaking is
complete, have taken a shape of its own, but even
so, the students can then shape it by pressing down
as in figure two. This latter technique largely
resembles the flipping method employed in "tiddly
winks." Many glass shards come from this step in
the process, so caution the students. You may wish
to draw up some basic designs of conventional
arrowheads (more accurately they are miniature
spearpoints), such as those in figure three. At
first, this process is difficult, but have the
student stay with it for some three class periods
and they will begin mass-producing these once they
get the feel for it. The boys generally have more
immediate success with this project as they usually
possess more hand strength. As a coaching point,
try to have the students flake deeply into the

glass, at a flatter angle, to obtain bigger chips (see figure five). It is more difficult, but the result is better. See how the angle of the screwdriver in figure four compares with the angle in figure five. The latter will produce a better spearpoint.

Other projects in this unit on prehistoric technology would include the making of shelltools and the painting of stelae. To make shelltools, of course the first item of need is a bag of sea shells, several dozen. Although the project is messy, it is simple. Have the students bang on the protrusion, or hinge, of the shell with a smooth hammerstone; then they can chip away at the edges to achieve any of the shapes conventionally found in shelltool cultures. Tell the kids not to worry about the mess and the volume of shell shards - the Penobscot Indians have left slag heaps along river banks in Maine several miles long and as much as ten feet deep. Not every shell yields a tool, obviously. The typical shapes are as follows:

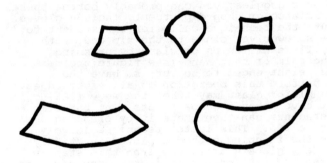

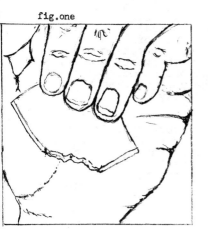

fig.one

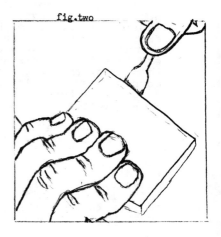

fig.two

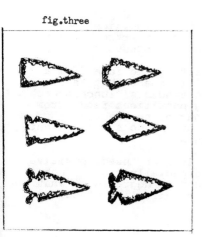

fig.three

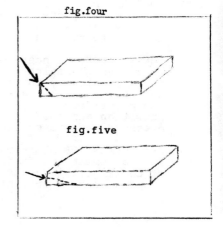

fig.four

fig.five

artwork by B.Patterson

To paint stelae, have the kids bring in shale, slate, or brick -- any large rocks with smooth surfaces. They can copy actual works of prehistoric art (i.e., cave paintings from Cro-Magnon Man, hieroglyphics from the Maya or Egyptian cultures, Hopi sand paintings, or any other works of aboriginal art) from photocopies that you supply or display. Have them outline their work with pencil or chalk (early man did this by scratching his etchings into stones smeared with animal grease) and then color them with conventional model paint. Of course, when this is all done you may wish to display the work in school or bury them for archaeological excavation.

95. PLAYS: Have the students work out socio-dramatic plays depicting the mentality of people living in different countries during different times. Such plays can serve to show students the origins of World War I, the heated issues of pre-Civil War slavery, South African apartheid, or the origins of the Cold War. Students can work up their own scripts in study groups; you would then edit and coordinate.

96. USE THE NEWS: Use the average local newspaper for such projects as current events, editorial writing, job searches for career classes, marketing samples for business classes, stock market analysis, and so on.

97. HOLD AN ART SHOW: Each year our art department holds an art show in the cafeteria in which they display, and sometimes sell, student artworks. It is easy to run and a highlight for students.

98. LUNCH CHECK: I heard of an intriguing idea from a grade school health teacher. It seems that this teacher actually inspects his students' lunches each day to see if they are eating nutritious foods from the major food groups. Of course, he teaches nutrition and food groups before he does this. What pressure he puts on the parents!

99. DEVELOPMENT OF SELF-CONCEPT: Everyone needs positive reinforcement and feedback, especially kids. Much of their self-image is enhanced or degraded by what happens to them in school. Academically, of course,

you will have the bulk of the input, but there are little things that can be done to make students aware of their own worth, values and self-image. Much of this thinking is best expressed in a book by Jack Canfield and Harold C. Wells entitled <u>100 Ways to Enhance Self-Concept in the Classroom</u> (Prentice-Hall, 1976). This is especially germane to those of you who teach elementary school, but the idea is to give students more chances to express their thoughts about themselves. Have them write auto-biographical sketches, draw self and family portraits, paste collages of things they like to do and to think about, write essays about their favorite past-time and interests, express their likes and dislikes on paper, and list their five most positive and five most negative traits. Fifth-grade teacher Mary Van Wickle selects two students per month for recognition on her classroom bulletin board. The chosen ones are asked to bring in items that they hold dear and show something about themselves. My own son brought in his hockey jersey, a trophy, a photo, etc. Positive self-concept is of course directly proportional to positive feedback -- the pat on the back, the congratulatory note, the public recognition for good work. You as a teacher can do a lot for any student's self-image, either subtly or overtly.

100. STUDENT OF THE WEEK: Why not select a student, praise his good works, and put them up on the bulletin board as the Student of the Week? Perhaps even put a picture up. Base the choice on academic or athletic endeavors, anything to emphasize the positive.

101. ONE HUNDRED QUESTIONS TO DEFINE A CULTURE: I once had a college student ask for my help on an assignment. Her task was to come up with one hundred questions that would indicate the values, mores, sanctions, and institutions that help shape a person's culture. This is a good reinforcement assignment for a sociology or anthropology class.

102. GYM CLASS LEAGUES: Kids thrive on competition. If you teach physical education, divide your class into basketball, softball, soccer, flag football, and field hockey classes. Keep the teams constant, give

them names, work up a schedule, post the standings, and watch the kids go at it like they are in playoffs. And, by the way gym teachers, never have students choose their teams in line-up fashion. Take it from an old last-picked "athlete" ...it hurts. Have the teams chosen randomly by counting down the line or out of a hat. If there is an imbalance, balance up the skill levels before play starts.

103. MODEL CONGRESS: Any history or civics class can employ this technique. Have each student research a state that he or she will represent as an interest in your model congress. Pick a Speaker of the House and recorders if possible. Select two issues and call for the introduction of each issue as a bill, send it through the entire process of committee, debate and role-call vote. Be very careful in choosing the issue to be voted on; be sure that it will reflect interests in the states you have represented. Furthermore, allow "deals," log-rolling, pork barrel riders, and so on -- just like the real thing. Appoint minority and majority whips as well as political party membership for each congressman. Allow partisan or bi-partisan voting and block voting.

104. THE ERRONEOUS STATEMENT: Offer extra-credit to the student who can pick out the factual error you intentionally make in a lecture. Be sure to inform the students at the end of the period which statement is flawed otherwise it will appear as an answer on a test! This can help spark attentiveness to the classroom presentation.

105. MEMORY-RETRIEVAL CLUES: Work with students to assist their memories. Acronym sequences, mnemonics, catch-words and phrases, and blend-in word sequences can be developed as a class for those long lists of terms, elements, names and so forth that can be tedious.

106. CONTESTS: Periodically hold essay, poetry, or project contests within your own class or throughout the school. Prize offerings can come from a variety of sources: the Board of Education, the Parent-Teacher Organization, local merchants or even generous parents. Prizes themselves can range from ballgame tickets to free lunch, from movie passes to

gift certificates. And of course, publicly praise and recognize the winners.

107. ASSEMBLY PROGRAM: Why not have your class conduct and sponsor an all-school assembly program? Of course, the subject material must be something that the entire school can benefit from and relate to. Have health classes conduct a program on drug or alcohol abuse. Have the science students present something on energy. Have forensic classes present a debate on a current public issue. You can also group certain interest fields together, such as all history students viewing an important documentary film or all journalism classes hearing a guest speaker from a major newspaper. Do not hesitate to share your films and speakers in general.

108. THE "SPEAKER-A-MONTH" LECTURE SERIES: Depending upon the nature of the course(s) you teach and the maturity and receptivity of your students, it might be worthwhile to try to line up a lecture series of monthly speakers on various topics of academic or social concern. The speakers can be drawn from the community, student's parents or relatives, or fellow teachers. Topics could be anything that might make things more interesting for the kids in your classroom -- use your imagination. It would not be inappropriate to pass out a questionnaire for students to take home at the beginning of the school year. On it you could describe your "Speaker-a-Month" concept and solicit input, possible speaker leads, etc.

109. MORAL DILEMMA QUESTIONS: When teaching a unit on prejudice or discrimination in whatever class might be applicable, run of a series of questions such as: how they would handle a situation where their daughter is marrying a man of another race, or suppose they find out their child is homosexual, or they witness an old man being beaten up in park by three hoodlum youths, or suppose while working as a security guard in a grocery market, they spy an improvished elderly woman attempting to steal a packet of meat that is obviously a long-overdue meal. Posing questions like these can make for an interesting, provocative class the next day when you discuss them. I have used the following assignment

131

sheet in teaching a social problems class about prejudice, discrimination, and ethnocentric thinking.

SOCIAL PROBLEMS CASE STUDIES:

Discrimination

CASE I: You are a 47-year-old parent of a son who is away at college. You know that he has been dating a girl quite seriously for sometime, yet you have not seen her. He writes that they are coming home this weekend so that he might introduce her to you and your wife. They walk in the door. She is of another race. The son announces that they plan to marry.

CASE II: You are an employer. Your company is hiring foremen for a construction job. You have five applicants for one job -- four are black and one is white. Your interviews boil the applicants down to one black and one white applicant. According to Affirmative Action mandates, you must hire the black foreman because you need more minorities on your staff. The white applicant is clearly more qualified. Which person do you hire?

CASE III: You are a judge in a criminal court. Your district is inner city where at least one-half of the population is made up of minorities. A 19-year-old man accused of burglary comes before your bench. He has been brought up twice before for the same offense. He operates during the day when no one is home and he is unarmed. He is black. That same day a 19-year-old white male who has burglarized a home at night and shot the homowner with a handgun comes before you. This is his first offense; the homeowner was wounded. You have these options: a) give the same sentence.
                      b) give a suspended sentence.
                      c) both receive a year in jail.
                      d) the man with the hand-gun can receive an additional year in jail if you wish.

　　　　　　　　e) the man with the three
　　　　　　　　offenses can receive an
　　　　　　　　additional two years in jail
　　　　　　　　if you wish.

　　　　WHAT DO YOU DO?

110. CLASS GAME: CORPORATION BOARD: This idea was
     written up in a fine book entitled A Handbook for
     the Teaching of Social Studies by Dobkin, Fischer,
     Ludwig and Koblinger (Allyn & Bacon, 1985).
     Basically it calls for the class to act as a
     corporate board. You pose the questions regarding
     price - policy, promotions and mergers and they make
     the decisions. Create imaginative scenarios and this
     can be an interesting exercise in group decision-
     making.

111. CLASS GAME - VIGILANTES: Another idea from the
     publication mentioned above. It calls for the class
     to either judge make-believe police in a crisis-
     intervention scenario or to make policy in the
     manner described above.

112. LEGAL BRIEFS: Law and Social Problems classes can
     benefit from your copying briefs of key, landmark
     decisions from the various state, federal, and
     appellate courts. Give them the circumstances of
     the cases, discuss them and then give the court
     findings and reasoning. I recommend that this be
     employed with upper level classes only.

113. CLASS GAME - LABOR MANAGEMENT: Divide the class in
     half, one being union labor and the other being
     management. Set up a scenario and then pose
     questions of significant interest to both parties.
     Debate, discuss, and decide by compromise...or
     strike. This idea was presented in Leonard H.
     Clark's Strategies and Tactics in Secondary
     School Teaching (McMillan, 1969).

114. CLASS GAME - CREATION OF A MODEL SOCIETY: Students
     of any academic level can relate to this game. You
     establish a bleak scenario in which those in the
     room are the only known (to them) survivors of a
     nuclear attack. Pose problems for them in a quasi-
     socratic method. Examples would be food procurance,

care for the sick and incapacitated, labor division, laws and rules, aggressive or passive relations with foreign groups that you may encounter, social deviance, etc. As they hash out and shape this society, jot down the laws and decisions for analytical discussion afterwards. This takes about three days of class. It works well with the students in a round-table forum.

115. CLUSTERING: This technique can help students with associative thinking. It can also help in such skills as study and outlining. Basically stated, give students a key word in the center of a work-sheet and then have them list and surround that key word with concepts and ideas associated with it. An example from the study of history would be as follows:

```
                        476 a.d.
                           |
Fertile Cresent ─────── ANCIENT HISTORY ─────── Greeks
       /                 /           \                 |
Mesopotamia           Rome          Egypt          Classical
       /               /               \               |
Hebrews          Punic Wars         Pyramids       Trojan War
       /             /                  \               |
Bible              law                pharoahs       Persian War
                   /                                    |
                empire               Peloponnesian War
```

Clustering can easily be used in teaching science, English and so on. Begin with base concepts and proceed to relative matters.

116. SUBCULTURAL CHARACTERISTICS: When teaching sociology and cultures, illustrate the various components of society by viewing its subcultures. Hand the students a worksheet in which they select any of the subcultures you describe in your lesson and have them consider the traits relative to that cultural group. I offer the following structure:

Choose any subculture existing in the United States. Examine them from the following viewpoints:
        a) position or status in American society
        b) group composition and social structure
        c) dress and distinctive ornamentation

d) daily activities
e) differentiating values and goals
f) political orientation
g) distinctive language
h) religious preference

117. HALLOWEEN: If you have any history or literature classes, why not give either extra credit or make it an assignment that the students dress up as someone famous in history or as a character in literature?

118. TEACHING ABOUT HANDICAPS: To help students understand the problems faced and adjustments made by handicapped or elderly people, a very enlightening assignment can be to "handicap your students for a day" by having them tape together the fingers of a hand, wear an eye patch (or two), tape their mouth shut, wear swimmers' ear plugs, or even be confined to a wheelchair during school all day.

119. STUDENT-MADE TESTS: Have the students in your class each make up three, four, or five questions for an upcoming test or quiz. Reserve your right to pick and choose as well as rephrase. This helps students spot what to look for in their test study.

120. CLASS GAME - MEDIEVAL FAIR: Terry Dozier, National Teacher of the Year in 1985, presented this idea for World History classes. Put on a fair that might have been typical of the Middle Ages.   Make it complete with costumes, games such as archery juggling, chess, quoits, backgammon, staff wrestling and minstrels. Put on puppet shows and knights' sword play. This idea can be expanded to include science fairs, history fairs, humanities fairs and so forth.

121. REPORT-ON-A-COUNTRY: For current affairs, geography and history classes, have the students select one extant world country and then present a formal report on its politics, economy, problems and promise. Have them compile a travel brochure, map and collage poster depicting their nation's character. This might be tied in with the Model U.N. indicated earlier.

122. "WHEEL OF FORTUNE": Why not employ the popular T.V. game show in teaching literary works, authors, historical facts, and foreign language phrases and words?

123. "JEOPARDY" AND "MATCH GAME": These are two more T.V. game shows that can be utilized in the classroom with slight modifications. Tie them into history, English, science, and foreign language classes.

124. READING REINFORCEMENT: Diane Dismuke, in a leading education journal in 1985, indicated that elementary reading can be enhanced and reinforced with matching words to illustrations, forming clay letters, reading along with cassettes and picture tape books, and cutting and pasting letters and works from magazines.

125. LIBRARY DAY: Set aside one day for your students to see the operation of the library - how books are found, their location and the set-up of the card catalog. Students at virtually every level can benefit, no matter what the discipline. Research techniques, periodicals and microfilm should also be touched upon. Upper level classes can benefit from exposure to some of the key journals that exists in their fields, too.

126. SIMULATED SPACE SHUTTLE: A middle school in Oakland, N.J. came up with an intriguing idea. They built a simulated space shuttle in the school gym, "launched" it with carbon dioxide and dry ice, and had seven student-astronauts live in the shuttle for one week. Periodically they broadcast transmissions to the school's classrooms and they conducted experiments in the capsule, etc.

127. THE GREAT EGG EXPERIMENT: A health and physical education teacher at Manasquan High School, Mrs. Geryl Moore, employs a brilliant way to convey the responsibilities of parenthood to her Senior Sex Education class. She has the kids carry egg(s) around with them -- wherever they go in school -- for one full week. These eggs are named, clothed and bundled. They cannot be lost or damaged, left alone, or otherwise mistreated. Reportedly, there have been cases of "injury," "death," and even

"kidnapping" as a disgruntled junior once held an
egg for ransom. It makes for an interesting as well
as an eye-opening week.

128. MAPS WITH A TWIST: Devise unusual maps such as
those that might require students to spot purposely-
inserted errors, sports teams' cities, religions,
all rivers, cities and countries whose names are
colors, and so on. It can break the monotony of
mundane map-location work.

129. SEMINAR PAPER: Upper level academic classes can be
exposed to the idea of a seminar paper. Select an
overall topic and then assign each student in the
class some aspect of that topic to research and
write upon. Take time to agree about mechanics and
paper construction, too. The results can be an
interesting and informative chain of papers that can
tie together into a fine booklet. Suggestions might
range from the Romantic writers to the Jews in
history to watershed scientific experiments. I
have seen these papers published and the effect can
be positive for all involved.

130. WALL STREET: Give students a lesson in stock market
function by giving them an imaginary sum of money,
have them invest it in stocks, and then have them
follow their stocks' progress on the appropriate
pages of a newspaper. They can sell, trade, and
purchase more stock as they wish. When the lesson
is completed (by setting a particular date some
months hence), see who has made more money, who
has lost and why.

131. CEMETERY ASSIGNMENT: Dr. Ken Carlson, Rutgers
University, gives his social studies graduate
students a unique assignment - visit a graveyard to
learn what they can about a community. It can be a
surprising lesson as students realize community
values, compare social attitudes over time and even
learn of cultural prejudices.

132. ORIENTEERING - In teaching a class on geography or
geometry, orienteering with a compass can be an
interesting diversion. Compasses can be purchased
for under ten dollars. Instruct the class in their
use and operation. Having learned that, the

students can be brought outside the next class day
and put through an orienteering course that you have
set up on school grounds with cardboard placards
strategically placed. Hide them from plain view and
have the kids work in pairs. Offer a prize to the
first team to successfully complete the course
without getting lost. Have a slogan or symbol on
each placard so that you know, by viewing students'
notes taken during the outing,that they did, in
fact, visit each location.

133. NEWSPAPERS AND MAGAZINES: If your school system
allows you to purchase a class set of newspapers or
magazines, it can be interesting from the standpoint
of current events, yet problematic because of time
constraints. One way to work around this problem is
to set aside the first five minutes of each class
for reading time. This gives the class a full
twenty-five minutes over the course of the week and
it helps quiet the class down at the beginning of
each period. Pre-assign the articles you wish to
have them read.

134. THE LIVING BILL OF RIGHTS: Clip articles from the
newspaper which deal with civil rights matters such
as arrest, search and seizure; discrimination; etc.
After teaching the Bill of Rights, have students
read and express their views on these current cases.

135. TEACHING THE CONSTITUTION: Give out copies of the
document and read it with the class in a round-table
format. Break it down, discuss, define and apply.
It takes two to three weeks of class time, but is
well worth the effort. Conclude with a summary
notesheet.

136. LISTS: Modeled after Hart's Hundred listing of the
100 most significant people in world history,
students can benefit from producing their own
analytical lists of such things as the ten most
important wars, 50 most important events, 25 worst
people in history, ten most important scientific
discoveries, and so on. Even a revamping of Hart's
list can be interesting.

137. CLASS CHALLENGE: Why not have your class challenge
another teacher's class in a geography bee, a
spelling or math contest, or something of similar
nature? It need only take up a single class period

and the prizes could be as simple as ice cream from the school cafeteria.

138. FAMOUS PHOTOS: In teaching American History, run off copies of famous paintings and photographs for the sake of student identification.

139. CITY HALL ASSIGNMENT: In teaching political science or civics, assign the students a series of options dealing with local governance. Have them visit a municipal court in session or a boro council meeting; they might even interview the mayor. They can do this on their own time, but you might supply them with meeting dates and times. Discuss their observations in class.

140. MULTIPLE-CAUSES DIAGRAMMING: If you are teaching a unit or event such as a war, write up a handout with the event shown in the center of the page and radiate spokes like a wheel out from it. Have the students write in the causes which contributed to the event's occurrence. (Gagnon)

PART V:

DISCIPLINE

"If someone had told me that I would be Pope
one day, I would have studied harder."

John Paul I

"With discipline you are irresistible!"

George S. Patton

Aside from knowledge of subject material, the ability to conduct and maintain a disciplined classroom is probably the most important component of teaching. Indeed, the argument can be made that this is the most important aspect of teaching, for without discipline in the classroom, how can we impart knowledge? Furthermore, it is the area that supervisors look to first in evaluating teachers. Yet it is the one thing that we are often least prepared for.

One of the first rules of discipline is consistency. Avoid favoritism and administer justice fairly. Set rules and make them known. I have already spoken about the importance of passing out written classroom rules and regulations. In this way, if a student knowingly violates the rules, it is clear to all who is in the wrong and what the punishment should be. I once asked a high school vice-principal if disciplining students was a difficult job. He replied that it was not. He stood by his rules and the students knew them, him and the consequences. All children need structure and this is what rules and regulations provide.

It may seem contradictory, but the second rule of discipline is flexibility. A child may have a genuine and unique excuse. His home life is a mess; there may be a truly disturbing personal problem that has arisen. Flexibility and deviation from your rules, when appropriate, must be done in confidence, however. It is between you and the student in question. If you go public with this, you open yourself to charges of favoritism and you will soon begin to hear every excuse known to man come floating in with students to be disciplined.

The third rule, as I see it, is fairness. Caesare Beccaria once said, "Let the punishment fit the crime." Do not overkill with detentions and punishment assignments for the slightest infraction. There comes a point of diminishing returns in iron-handed discipline -- the more you mete out, the less respect you obtain and the more covert deviance you will encounter. Similarly, fairness means equality before the rules. Do not administer one set of rules for one child and another set of rules for another.

I try to handle all discipline myself, as stated earlier. I do not like to send students to the office.

This seems to be, as I see it , an admission of my own failure to discipline. Some students will act up just to get out of class. Do not give them what they want; do not make yourself look weak either to your students or to the administrators. However, if a student is truly disruptive, consistently obnoxious, and your methods are having no real effect, then do not hesitate to throw him or her out of your classroom and into the office.

Administrators, if any of you read this, it is imperative that you back your teachers. The child must know that the (Vice-) Principal's Office is the end of the line. Additionally, teachers must feel confident that the administration will support them. It works both ways; if a teacher does not abuse the practice of sending unruly students to the office, then the administrators are more apt to support them when they do send a child down. Nothing undermines a school system like a lack of coordinated discipline between the faculty and the administration.

Some general considerations in discipline cases might be as follows:

1. Isolate problem students -- move their seat(s), put them in the corner; this works especially well on the socialite, the talker.
2. Speak privately to the clownish student -- do not reinforce his attention - getting behavior; invariably, the clown likes to be chewed out by the teacher in front of the class. You scream and he smiles; he is the victor.
3. Speak singularly and privately to the "macho" student. This character, to salvage his challenged image, will come back at you in a confrontational tone if you deal with him in front of the entire class; also, always know exactly what you intend to say to this type, or any student, when confronting him or her alone.
4. To the student who regularly whines about fairness, one technique is to throw his case, if it is a poor one, out to the entire class for judgment; do this in a semi-mocking tone and they will usually laugh him or her out of "court."
5. To the note-passer, read the composition aloud to the class. Although I have heard of critics who say not to do this, I like to make a joke out of

the situation by not only reading the note
aloud, but adding in spicy tidbits as I read.
The note-passing usually stops. If the note is
especially filthy, however, sent it home to the
parents...or hold it as blackmail over the child
so that his performance improves.
6. To the students who like to pack up before the
dismissal bell is to ring you can either hold
them after the bell or have them jot down a late
addition to their notebook which you describe as
"crucial"...after they have packed things up, of
course.
7. For foul language, detention is my rule. I like
to describe my detentions as "long and often,"
although I admit that there is more bark than
bite here. Foul language might also be dealt
with by a note home to the parents.
8. Disrespect is handled by detention or by sending
the student to the office, depending upon how
open, blatant, and severe it is. Tolerate no
disrespect -- it can quickly erode your classroom
discipline.
9. Student fights: if they are only verbal, end
them with quick intervention, as verbal fights
often lead to more physical encounters. This
need be all that is done if both parties cease
and desist. For the physical fight, it is
usually school policy that the combatants be sent
to the office. Use discretion here. If the
fight looks like it may not go any further, you
may wish to warn both parties after breaking it
up and then let them go. But if it a potentially
on-going affair, send them to the office. In
either case, notify the office because a repeat
offense handled by someone else when you are not
around may only result in continued warnings.
Consider the students involved in the fight, too.
Is one or both of them a habitual belligerent?
Refer them to the office if so. By the way,
boys' fights are usually easier to break up than
girls' fights. Truly! Boys are often pushing
and shoving with one eye to the door, hoping
someone will intervene. They only "fought" to
protect their macho image anyway and their anger,
therefore, quickly abates. Girls, however, can
be particularly vicious, will often repeat their
encounter, and at times are the most difficult to
pry apart.

10. Impudence (a step down from disrespect) can best be handled by a private conference after class in which you drill your finger into the kid's chest. Detention or office referral, depending upon whether he/she gets the message is the remedy for this.
11. For the student who manifests a general lack of self-discipline, it may be difficult, but one approach is to try to channel him or her into a sport. Sports can provide the structure that his life needs and he is obviously not getting at home. It fills un-used, potentially troublesome hours, too.

You may note that I have not mentioned corporal punishment. I teach in New Jersey, one of only a few states that bans corporal punishment in schools. Although the merit of this policy is fuel for debate better handled elsewhere, it has served to make New Jersey's teachers more resourceful in terms of disciplining their pupils.

The aforementioned are by no means hard and fixed rules. The best advice is to use your professional judgment and consider each incident from as many angles as possible. Consider the future impact, the lesson learned by your discipline, the effect on the child's image (both within and without), and the effect on your image.

In most cases, try to get to the root of the student 's problem: why he acts as he does. Police have an old expression that well serves to analyze deviant behavior. They say that there are two kinds of jerks (I am using the more socially acceptable term here) in this world -- situational jerks and terminal jerks. We can all be situational jerks; the trick is to avoid being a terminal jerk. The teacher, like the cop, deals with both types, but unlike the cop, the teacher must see the classroom jerk every day. Therefore it behooves the teacher to try to modify the jerk's behavior in some way. The cop can punish, but the teacher must try to re-direct the jerk's course.

Speak to other teachers, observe the student in the hallway and lunchroom, speak to his guidance counselor. What is his homelife like? Is he heavily influenced by peers? What are his interests and values? Would getting him an after-school job or into a sport help structure his life? I have said it before that as teachers we must be social workers, psychologists, judges and juries, all rolled into one. Try to determine whether you are dealing with a terminal or situational jerk.

Teachers should be aware that we too, can have the rule of situational or terminal jerk applied to us. We must not be the cause of our own discipline problems. Among the things that can turn a class into behavioral deviants are these:

a) failure to adhere to consistent rules of discipline such as those outlined earlier.
b) wise-cracking without allowing reciprocity.
c) failing to vary the classroom presentation mode and atmosphere.
d) showing a lack of care, interest, or organization.
e) improper and unfair tests and assignments.
f) not listening to student needs, questions or concerns.
g) being a dictator, charlatan or pedant.

Although most of the aforementioned thoughts on discipline are derived from my own years in the class-room, I would like to paraphrase a selection from Alcorn, Kinder and Schunert who spoke of the Ten Commandments of Discipline in their <u>Better Teaching.</u>
1. Begin right -- set the proper classroom atmosphere.
2. Be businesslike.
3. Be alert.
4. Be tactful -- request rather than command.
5. Be cheerful.
6. Be just.
7. Be persistent.
8. Be consistent.
9. Be decisive.
10. Be judicious.

ABSENTISM AND DETENTION

Is there a relationship between student absenteeism, grades and overall deviant behavior? Yes, most definitely, as a study of 30,000 high school sophomores in 1981 by DiPrete, Muller and Shaeffer showed. They specifically looked at absenteeism, trouble with the law, cutting classes, lateness to school, and not doing homework. Here are the results, although they do not surprise us:

Types of Misbehavior	Mostly A's	Mostly B's	Mostly C's	Mostly D's
Avg. days absent per semester	2.28	2.99	4.20	7.87
Avg. days late per semester	2.05	3.12	4.41	6.44
Percentage of sample not doing assigned work	1.10	2.73	6.27	24.72
Percentage of sample who cut a class during school year	28.73	43.39	58.15	67.21
Percentage of sample in serious trouble with law	1.62	2.93	7.37	14.06

(Source: Discipline and Order in American High Schools, Wash., D.C., 1981)

Since so many of these students are seen in detention, let me offer a quick piece of advice: make detention meaningful. If these students have any delinquent homework assignments, tell them they will not be dismissed until at least one late assignment is handed in. Or, if you have several things to get done such as filing, typing, cleaning up or the like, have them do it for you. Interestingly, students seem to respond positively to a negative situation when it is handled in this manner. Central Office detention? Have the student line the athletic fields, cut grass, even paint walls or clean up litter. Time, in any context, is too precious to waste.

TEN OF THE MOST COMMON STUDENT CHALLENGES

During the average week of high school or junior high school, you will encounter some, and more probably all, of these commonly found student challenges.
1. "I didn't know that assignment was due."
2. "You never mentioned that."
3. "If most of the class fails, then it's the teacher's fault."
4. "How am I doing, grade-wise?"
5. "What do I have to do to pass?"
6. "I can't find anything on that research topic."
7. "What am I missing for homework?"
8. "I have a test to make-up."
9. "Can I take a make-up instead of today's test?"
10. "How come I got a (C, D or F)?"

The key factor in all of these challenges is to not get flustered, defensive or confrontational. As can be seen, many of the charges are ridiculous and juvenile. They can be dismissed as exactly that -- smile and laugh them off. Give them a "raised eyebrow" or slough it off with a trite, "that's life." Be sure to size up the challenge accurately; the child may be seeking genuine help. Be sure to react appropriately.

Do not become defensive as the students will quickly see this as a sign of weakness. Remember that the best defense is a good offense. You have, or should have, the documentation and evidence to support your position. Merely fall back on your rules and numbers and the objectivity they afford.

The most critical element, I feel, is to avoid the confrontation. Teenagers have an abundance of pride, much of it misplaced. If you confront them or openly challenge them directly in the middle of the classroom, many of them will respond with emotion based on their ego rather than their logic. It is the malady of youth -- I have heard it referred to as the "paradox of irrationality." You can convey the confrontational message with an off-handed tone of voice, a shrug, and a wry smile. The child will get the message and you will not have to send him to the office for a reply that you might have forced him into. However, if there remains an issue that demands confrontation, have the student see you privately after class. Being up front with students does not always mean confronting them.

148

In addressing each of these questions or challenges, I believe that I have given you the answers to them throughout this volume, especially in my passage on classroom organization. Also realize that the younger the child, the better it is to specifically answer his complaint because the young ones often take your answer home to mom and dad.

Specifically, however, when told by the student he did not know something was due, I point to the roster sheet and the assignment listing. When told that I never mentioned something that was asked for on a test, I ask other students to check their notebooks. If even one student has written down the item in question, then I am right. Do not be so egotistical as to stubbornly cover up an error on you part. Either throw out the question or give them all credit for it if, in fact, the material was not covered. If a student tells you that since most of the class fails a test it's the teacher's fault, I reply with the idea that if everyone passed, it would not be a true test, just a simple worksheet. You can further beef this up with the suggestion that you have given this test before and other classes have passed it. However, once again be sure that the student is not correct -- is it indeed your fault that they all failed? Check your test and teaching method as they pertain to that unit.

To the ubiquitous, "How am I doing?", ask them if all of their work is in. Answer them with a pass-fail response. Do not tie yourself into a specific grade as this may come back to haunt you, especially with a student who is working to just get by satisfactorily. If you tell him he has a C, he may take the remainder of the marking period off, end up with a D or F and then blame you for misleading him. If he wants a more specific response, either deny the request outright or offer him extra credit to help him boost his way toward his goal-grade. Do not feel that you are remiss here. You cannot be expected to have all work graded at every instance during the marking period, nor can you take time from the class to continually average individual student grades. You may wish to set aside a certain time of day and have the student see you then, but this is up to you. The similar question is "What do I have to do to pass?" I tritely reply with this truism: "Get all your work in on time." In many cases that alone will do the trick.

"I can't find anything on that topic" is a favorite. Students doing research seem to think that magically a book will jump off the shelf and address their specific topic. Sometimes the book exists; most often it does not. This challenge can be tough. A good reply is to offer other angles that the student may not have considered. Shift their topic in another direction; re-define it. Suggest tangents.

When asked what they are missing in homework assignments, point to the roster sheet. When asked about making up a test, you may try to accommodate their schedule, but if you and the student simply cannot coordinate the times, then have the student make up your test during any of your classes, excluding the one he has the test in. If his period six is open with a study hall but you have a class, he can stop in then and take it in the back of the room. This should work, but if it is inappropriate for perhaps obvious reasons, you may have to insist upon pre-school or post-school time. To this, you may get the reply, "But I have to work after school." Tell the student that the choice is his; put the pressure on the student's shoulders. It may be appropriate to remind students that their first job, at this point in their life, is education.

A favorite inquiry is "Can I take a make-up test?" Sometimes the student will hit you with this one as he is looking at the test you have just passed out. I lay down the rule that once they see the test, they must take it. More often, this question will pop up just prior to the test or quiz being administered. I simply check their absences. Only an absence on the day before a test is permissible, generally speaking. I am flexible for such things as extended periods of absence, however. In all cases, moreover, I tell them outright that the make-up test is more difficult.

The final challenge - how come I got an F, D or C -- is almost inevitable. It is a sound practice to take the time both at the beginning and at the end of the marking period to explain how the grades are arrived at. In this way, you can head off many of these inquiries. Often times, it simply takes some specific, individualized time. If you have been fair and kept accurate records, you usually win. If you are wrong, do not be afraid to change the grade. It is more important to be fair and accurate than it is to simply look good.

I usually like to take some classtime midway through a
marking period and call out homework points and quiz
points accumulated to that point. It helps focus
student achievement. I submit that high school students
usually have a sense of what their grade status is...
they only tell their parents that they had no idea they
were doing so poorly.

STUDENT DEFENSE MECHANISMS

I noted at the beginning of this book that one of
the roles of the teacher is that of the psychologist.
With that in mind, and because of the layman's
fascination I have for the theories of Sigmund Freud, I
offer this primer on ego defense mechanisms. Actually
all of us employ some (hopefully not all) of these
gambits in our everyday lives. Students are no
different and you can be sure that you will encounter
the full range.

PROJECTION: Freud says that when a person knows
that he is wrong or guilty, he often transfers that
guilt to someone else. Two contrasting examples would
be, "Tommy made me do it," or " I hate her" actually
referring to "She hates me."

DISPLACEMENT: When a student is angered or
frustrated he may shift his aim to some other object.
Examples would be vandalism or settling for something
rather than seeking their true aim.

REPRESSION: This is probably Freud's favorite
starting point in analyzing a person. Repression deals
with the idea that there are hidden and suppressed
urges, memories or feelings within us. These drives all
seek outward expression, but because of their social
unacceptability, they can only gain manifestation in a
disguised or altered form. Hostility toward parents,
for example, may force a child to be disruptive in
school. The jealousy a boy has for his sister may take
the form of picking on female classmates.

REGRESSION: Freud felt that all people grow through
various stages in their psychological maturation.
Regression refers to the idea that a person may revert
back to an early stage. For example, a third-grader
under some hidden stress or unsure how to cope with the
new pressures about him may revert back to bed-wetting

or thumb-sucking. Daydreaming or impulsive behavior
fall into this category, too.

   FIXATION: This occurs when a person remains fixed
at one level in his psychological growth. Simply
stated, this could be called immaturity; for example, a
college senior whose only priorities are cars, sex,
music and parties. Many times fixation occurs because
of a fear of failure. In either case, anxiety seems to
be the fore-runner of fixation.

   IDENTIFICATION: This occurs when a person idolizes
or wishes to be like another person and seeks to emulate
him or her through dress, speech, values and mannerisms.
Narcissism and hero-worship fall into the realm of
identification. Whereas identifying with admired people
is in most cases normal, it is not always healthy if
carried to an extreme. Look at the person the student
is seeking to be like. It may reflect a need, a gap in
his life, or an inability to deal with his emerging
self. In some ways displacement or projection can be
the opposite of identification; in many cases,
identification can be symptomatic of a poor self-image.

   SUBLIMATION: This is the transference of hidden
drives, desires, and feelings into socially acceptable
channels. A child may be a great athlete because of a
need to get his father to recognize him. Cigarette
smoking may be an expression of thumb-sucking
insecurity.

   REACTION-FORMATION: This occurs when one urge or
instinct is hidden by the opposite expression. For
example, purity may hide perversion, altruism may hide
selfishness, love may even hide hate. Denial can often
hide want. Freud may be on shaky ground here, but this
theory can apply to some individuals.

   RATIONALIZATION: This is perhaps the most widely
known and utilized of Freud's ego defense mechanisms,
for when one rationalizes, he or she projects reasons as
to why actions are taken or not taken. Procrastination,
alibis and excuses enter into this aspect of Freudian
theory.

   Having some awareness of these basic defense
mechanisms can help in your assessment and diagnoses of
what makes a child act the way he or she does.

PROBLEMS KIDS FACE

A discussion of discipline would be incomplete
without some insights into what problems children face
that may cause or at least add to their deviant
behavior. I have already alluded to the myriad of
general peer pressures, home life and societal
expectations that all work to confuse the maturation
process. On an individual basis, these maladies may be
relatively easy to detect through observation and
talking to colleagues, counselors, and so on.

Perhaps it is an aside, but did you ever stop to
contemplate the position we place our adolescents in?
On one hand they are told to "grow up," "act your age"
and then they are told "no, you are not old enough for
that." We, as a society, do pose problems for our
teenagers in terms of their parameters and boundaries.
Other, so-called "primitive" societies have ceremonies
such as rites of passage in which teens often undergo
painful ordeals to be recognized as adults. Once
passing the prescribed tests, however, they are fully
accepted in to adult status. These rites of passage may
occur as early as twelve or thirteen years of age. The
closest things we have to such rites are graduation,
confirmation and marriage - hardly painful ordeals, but
that does depend upon your point of view. As a result
of the lack of definition of teen status in America, our
adolescents grope for symbols of adulthood such as
smoking, drinking and sexual bravado. However, these
may or may not be the cause of deviant behavior, but
merely experimentation or ego identification.

However, what of the truly disruptive influences
over a child that are often the hardest to detect and
are most often beyond the ability of the child to cope
with? I of course refer to child abuse, sexual abuse
and drug/alcohol abuse. There is no lack of literature
on these subjects, to be sure, but what I offer here is
a simplistic overview of the things that the teacher can
look for. These items are not often mentioned in
education books, but I feel they are critical. My
information is garnered from many sources on the subject
and can serve as a synopsis of things for the classroom
teacher to look for. This information can help in
parent conferences, too. These are the truly tragic
cases that must be dealt with directly, not ignored or
glossed over.

SYMPTOMS OF CHILD ABUSE: It is generally accepted
that there are four types of child abuse falling under

the umbrella classification of the Battered Child Syndrome (BCS). The first, physical neglect includes the lack of basic care such as heat, food, clothing, medicine, shelter and hygiene. Emotional neglect is the lack of love, warmth and praise. Physical abuse is commonly associated with BCS and it includes beatings and actual torture. The emotionally abused child is constantly screamed at and has serious problems with self-identity and self-esteem. Symptoms to look for are bruises and lacerations on a consistent basis, an overt clinging toward sympathetic adults, general withdrawal, repetitive excuses, extremely aggressive behavior (his parents have served as a role model), unusual-type bruises (teeth marks and rope burns), a reluctance to go home, wearing clothing that covers bruised areas when the weather might not dictate their propriety, or if you are extremely lucky, a straight-out plea for help from the afflicted child. Also look for changes in appetite, grooming, basic health care, excessive shyness toward adults, and so forth. Do not be naive -- they are out there. Well over 625,000 cases of child abuse occur each year and these are only the reported cases; some estimates suggest figures of over one million per year.

SYMPTOMS OF SEXUAL ABUSE: Look for an unwillingness to participate in gym classes, withdrawal, unprovoked crying, anorexia, precocious sexual knowledge or behavior, runaway tendencies, suicide attempts, excessive fear of male adults, difficulty walking or standing, pain or itching in the genital areas, chronic visits to the nurse and unaccounted-for hours after school.

Other things to look for in abused children in general are poor nutrition, fatigue, excessive freedom from parental constraints, poor school attendance, speech disorders, failure to thrive, substance abuse, a reluctance to talk about family life and personal problems, and a general lack of parental involvement in either the school activities or their child's life. Parents are ubiquitous in the lives of elementary school children, so an "invisible parent(s)" might be cause for some immediate concern. Parental involvement does dissipate during the high school years.

SYMPTOMS OF ALCOHOL AND DRUG ABUSE: Look for sudden changes in values and schoolwork, changes in friends and associates, unkempt or neglected appearance, fatigue, withdrawal from active social life including sports, recreation and so on, bragging about their party nights

and "tying one on," alcohol-related incidents such as
DWI (Driving While Intoxicated) violations, fighting, a
unusual need for money, excessive thirst, the smell of
alcohol or strong odor of perfumes or breath fresheners,
general disaffection, emulation of drug-associated rock
stars and role models, parents who drink excessively*, a
small tight-knit circle of friends, tell-tale body signs
such as needle marks, blood vessel "track lines," an
inordinate possession and/or flaunting of money,
sunglasses at inappropriate times, a generally unhealthy
appearance, unaccounted-for hours and the cutting of
classes.

A recent trend in drug abuse occurs in athletes
using steroids. While the academic teacher might have
little opportunity to observe steroid abuse, gym
teachers would see it first. Obviously, sudden muscle
growth is an indicator, but look for a "bloated," watery
look to the muscles; a deepened voice and more
aggressive, almost enraged over-reactive behavior
patterns are other tell-tale signs.

SYMPTOMS OF SUICIDAL TENDENCIES: An excellent rule
of thumb to keep in mind here is the most obvious one -
if anyone you know ever hints, contemplates, or openly
discusses suicide, then you must respond. Most suicides
are forewarned. Untroubled people do not discuss such
things in reference to their own lives. As it concerns
children, all of the aforementioned problems and their
characteristics apply, as suicide is seen as the final
solution. Add to the list such ideas as "sign-off
behavior" such as giving away possessions, high-risk
behavior in which a hitherto conservative person
suddenly exhibits daredevil bravado, and insidious and
overt themes of death depicted in art and essays.

In all cases where you observe the signs of
potential child abuse in random combination, deal with
it; do not close your eyes or dismiss it. Talk to
peers, counselors, colleagues, churchmen, police,
administrators and perhaps even parents directly. Most
states have some sort of help "hot-lines" for social
work agencies and their phone numbers are listed in the
telephone book, the local newspaper or with the police.
If you suspect it, report it. You do not need to prove
it -- that is for the authorities.

---

*One remarkable study showed that in 90 percent of the
homes where parents did not drink, their children
followed suit almost to the same percentage; in 90
percent of the homes where parents did drink, their
children did, too.

A final thought on discipline is that it is the responsibility of everyone involved in the education process. First and foremost in this process is the teacher in his or her classroom and that we have already tried to establish in this portion of the text. Secondly it is the responsibility of the school administration to back its teachers. This is fundamental and has been alluded to earlier. Thirdly, the parents play a key role. When you send a poor test, a failure note or some other memo home, it is fair to ask, "What is being done to back you up on the home front?" Call the parents in if need be. But do not be naive; no matter what you do, there will still be parents who could not care less about their child's welfare. All too often, they are the first to criticize the school, too. Fourthly, discipline is the responsibility of the legal system and the police. Consider the results of this alarming set of statistics from the New York City Police Department: 1,635 guns, knives and other weapons were found in New York City schools in 1984 and there were 2,730 attacks, assaults, and other crimes committed against teachers in that system in 1982. Plainly stated, those "students" culpable should be removed from the public schools. It was once said that education is a privilege, not a right. Abuse of the privilege infringes on other students and teachers, so the abusers should be removed and either placed in educational facilities outside of the conventional school or not allowed in until they can demonstrate self-control and social restraint.

PART VI

MOTIVATION

"All life is based on the fact that
anything worth getting is hard to
get...The world is full of people
who have missed their destiny
because they would not pay the
price."

William Barclay

"Above all, a student should look for
-- and expect to find -- professors who
can bring to life the subject at hand."

William J. Bennett

The ability to motivate is like the ability to run fast -- either you have it or you don't. Before you become discouraged, however, I feel that the ability to motivate is a skill that can at least be enhanced.

Motivation is directly proportional to enthusiasm. You must enjoy your job. The higher the energy level you possess, the more charged your classroom atmosphere is and the more motivated everyone becomes. It has been said that excitement is contagious. I will discuss how to radiate this excitement in your classroom, during your lectures, and in your professional demeanor.

Components of motivation include enthusiasm not only on the part of the teacher, but also in the atmosphere of the classroom.Look around the classroom you might presently be in. Is it drab, lackluster? Picture it as your classroom. Now make it an extension of yourself with posters, bulletin boards, motivational slogans, and so on. I like to think of my classroom as my office. I have plants, magazines, charts, artwork, typewriter, paper trays and other trappings of business-like decor. I have even toyed with the idea of an aquarium. I have set aside tables for exhibits of a museum-like nature with student projects, artifacts and so on.

Another component of motivation is to show the student that you care. Although it sounds trite, we must remember that on the high school level, two issues manifest themselves. One, we all get carried away with our subject material -- the academics can supplant the student. This is not altogether wrong, but it can be carried too far so that we end up teaching in a manner oblivious to the students. Secondly, we must remember that our students are adolescents and they are often in need of some direction, assistance, role models and concern. Many times these children are searching for something, if not someone. Show them that you care. Little things like a student study guide can help demonstrate your interest in them. Take time for extra help; a telephone call or even a passing inquiry in the hallway may be remembered by the student. You never know when some small gesture like this reaches a child.

I have already referred to the posting of grades and assignments and this is one of the many components that can motivate students to achieve, although there are colleagues and parents who might find this objection-

able. I have found it effective with junior high school
and high school students. To carry this a step further,
I stumbled upon another idea a few years ago that
yielded some surprising results. I posted separately
the names of those students who earned the grade of A
under the listing of "Mr. T's A-team" (of course, the
analogous acronymic last name helped). Similarly, those
who failed the marking period were ignominiously listed
as belonging to the "F-Troop." At first I had
trepidations, not fully sure how high school students,
with their self-imposed sophistication, would react. I
was surprised. The A-team reacted with visible and
audible pride. Furthermore, I heard positive comments
from parents, so the message was brought home. On the
other hand, F-troop members reacted with embarrassment
and worked to get off the list. There even a request
for a B-team listing, but I turned that down.
Interestingly enough, after three years of posting these
lists, I found a definite and sustained decline in the
number of students who found their names on the F-troop.
Conversely, the A-team listing had grown. It may seem
radical, but it seems to work.

     Elementary school teachers have long been masters at
utilizing bulletin board space for motivation by posting
good student work, lists of "books read," stars for good
behavior each day, and so on. Teachers of all levels
can benefit from this age-old method, but with proper
modification.

     To facilitate motivation, gear projects that will
pique the students' interest. As an example, I have
assigned oral reports on famous disasters. The
historical significance may be minimal, but the
motivation to do research is positive. I actually heard
one marginal student say, "Hey, this could be fun" as he
was assigned a report of the San Francisco Earthquake
and his buddy was to report on the sinking of the
"Titanic."

     The contract method is another form of motivation.
Contrary to what some theorists would have you believe,
not every child sitting before you in the classroom is a
born intellectual fountainhead just waiting to be
tapped. Realistically, there are some students who
attend school simply because they must be there. For
classes of lower academic enthusiasm, but with a
smattering of highly motivated students, the pupil

contract method can work. Basically, the idea calls for a higher grade to be given for more work done. Establish the criteria, write them down, and pass them out to the students before-hand to avoid misunderstanding. A copy of the grade criterion given to your department chairperson would not hurt either. A typical contract system might call for those students wishing to earn an A to submit a ten-page, typed term paper complete with footnotes and bibliography. For a B, the student must submit a 1,000-word book review and for a C, the student would have to turn in two written summaries of television shows dealing with an approved, recommended topic.

Furthermore, in the contract system there should be a test percentage requirement. These should be based on average rather than a baseline cutoff score of, for example, "...no one scoring below 90 on any test can get an A." By averaging tests, the student is always motivated to score higher or at least maintain a good average as opposed to giving up after not doing well on one particular test. Typically, A-students should score 90 or better; B-students should average 83 or higher and C-students 75 or higher. Of course, this should be modified to adapt to your school's grading system.

Also specify that the students turn in all regularly assigned work.

On a cautionary vein, indicate that merely turning in any old thing for their written project does not automatically qualify them for an A, B or C. Specify that there are no guarantees. The work must be of A, B or C quality. Do not set any criteria for a grade of D, or barely passing, as this allows for too small a margin of error and would be theoretically counter-productive. I have seen teachers who actually write up a contract with the letter-grade goal and have the students sign it. Be sure that you have some record of what the student opts for.

Can a student striving for an A and doing all the appropriate work fall short and end up with a B or C? Yes, by not obtaining the appropriate grade average on tests and assignments. Make sure that the students understand this. Can a student obtaining an A average on tests but only doing the written work requirement for a B obtain an A? No, unless he or she turns in the A assignment.

Liberal use of extra credit work is a good motivator. Everything from written summaries of media presentations to typing up your worksheets and handouts related to the subject area to making charts that would enhance your classroom surroundings can be used. Throw in an extra five or ten points on their overall homework grade. Many students jump at the chance for such extra credit, especially at the end of the marking period. However, I stipulate that all regularly assigned work be in and that students see me for extra work -- I do not chase them down.

Vary your assignment types. Students hate to outline chapters from the text, but I see it as a necessary evil and therefore assign it. However, outlining and end-of-chapter text questions cannot be the only types of assignments you give. Your course will quickly become stale, your homework burdensome, and your motivation level will drop. For homework, give the students crossword puzzles, maps, logic problems, trivia assignments, art work, political cartoons, wordgrams, newspaper articles, simulated newspaper front pages depicting certain eras in history, dioramas, hands-on scientific experiments, you-are-there essays, and so on as far as your imagination can conceive. I have detailed these items earlier. Simply remember that a student may dislike one type of assignment but may respond to another type.

Just as importantly, vary the presentation. I have dealt with this earlier in my comments on effective lecturing, but try to present your material from as many different angles as possible and utilize as many different methods as possible. Films, tapes, oral lecture, use of the overhead projector, guest speakers, oral reports, assigned readings and so forth can be used to supplement the daily presentation that, no matter how enthralling you may be, students turn off eventually. Presentation modes should be varied from class-to-class even within the same course so that students at different learning levels can be reached. However, be aware of the need for a certain structure of material content as you may be inclined, with varied present- ations, to forget some items within your coverage. In other words, no matter how well you know your material, you still need lecture notes, at least in skeleton form, to be glanced at occasionally.

When presenting films to class, there are several ways to stimulate student attentiveness. Pass out question sheets before-hand that they must fill is as the film progresses. Forewarn them of a quiz at the end of a film. Have them write a review essay of specific content after the film or a simply have them take notes during the film. All too often, films in class mean lights out mentally as well as environmentally.

Kenneth H. Hoover, in The Professional Teachers Handbook (Allyn & Bacon, 1976), suggests dividing the class time into segments of fifteen minutes each wherein students might read material, hear a lecture or see a short film, and then discuss or review. Realizing that student attention time is not always attuned to a forty-five minute classroom presentation, this method might help keep the lesson in focus. Segmenting the class time would be particularly important for younger classes and lesser motivated and/or weaker learners.

Another facet in motivation is to "ice the cake." By this I mean a public recognition of outstanding work. If your school does not have a fine arts or literary magazine, start one. This is different from the school newspaper and much easier to publish. This publication solicits artwork, essays, poems, short stories, term papers, book reviews and award-winning efforts from any and all school departments and teachers. It takes a minimal amount of time. Simply organize the submitted material, judge and accept or reject, have student editors re-type when necessary, copy the material on school copying machinery, collate and distribute. The student response can be surprising. Similarly, create a special section of either the school library or your room resource area for research papers of scholarly merit. These can be drawn upon by future students in their own research. They should be properly credited in bibliographies and indeed, the paper's bibliography can be of significant value to other students. I have always felt it injudicious to throw away good papers; however, I am very select as to what papers get into this file. They truly must be the cream of the crop.

To motivate, it is important to remember that you must take the initiative and lead by example. It has been said that motivation begins from the top and works downward; rarely does it proceed from the bottom upwards.

Positive reinforcement is perhaps the soundest motivational device in existence. It can also be the easiest to implement. To understand what positive reinforcement is, one must realize what characterizes negative reinforcement. To be the type of teacher who is constantly yelling and screaming at the class, who regularly emphasizes the poorer qualities in a student, who uses grades as punishment, and who rarely offers a little pat on the back is the kind of teacher who will not get maximum returns from his or her pupils. Although initially effective, all the yelling and screaming is eventually turned of by the students and all of the negative personal aspersions can become self-fulfilled prophecies.

Positive reinforcement is simply the opposite behavior pattern. Offer praise, call out A and B grades for deserving students when returning papers, send home notes indicating positive classroom behavior, utilize the media forms noted earlier. Do not take good work for granted -- find ways to reward it. Call students to the front of the room after class and tell them they are doing a nice job. Try the old carrot-and-stick approach, too. For example, I have told classes that if everyone in the class passes the upcoming test, I will count it double. That has yet to happen. To be sure, there are many times when you need to shake up a class or a student or "tell it like it is" in a private meeting or in a letter home to a parent, but these instances should never numerically surpass the positive rewards. If they do, you might be headed toward an unbridgeable gulf between you and your students.

Let me offer some contrasting examples of negative and positive handling of identical situations.

Situation I:

    Negative: "It's about time you got an A on a test in this class, Billy!"

    Positive : "Hey, gang, Billy scored an A on this test -- one of the highest grades in the class!"

Situation II:

    Negative: "If you don't turn in a book report, I"ll see to it that you fail!"

    Positive: "A decision on your part to not turn in a book report will certainly mean that you can't earn higher than a C grade this marking period, if that. I'll do all I can, but you've got to do the work."

Situation III:

    Negative: "Al, are you stupid? Are you lazy? Get your work in and do a better job on it!"

    Positive: "Al, what's the problem here? Your work is usually late and poorly done. Is there something I can help you with? I'll tell you what, get all of your back work in on Monday and I won't send home the failure notice, O.K.?"

You can see how the same message is conveyed, but the student walks away from each encounter feeling substantially different. It is up to you to make the encounter a positive motivational device.

It is easy to motivate good students -- they make us all look good . It is the task of the teacher to motivate the marginal and poorer student. No teacher can reach every kid; it is simply an impossibility. Some students, for whatever reasons, are disaffected and simply will not perform academically. They may have no direction at home; they may have other interests in their lives that are more important than school. However, there is that borderline majority of students that you should work toward in your motivational endeavors. Note that I said majority -- I mean just that. Although the figures most certainly vary from school to school and from class to class, perhaps 15 percent of your class will fall into that highly motivated group that will work for an A grade no matter what you do. Then there is the group of some 5 percent who will do nothing and could not care less about it.

Of course, we should try very hard to reach the latter people, but we cannot blame ourselves if we fail. That leaves some 80 percent of the class that may earn any grade between D or B, often depending upon motivation.

In stimulating the poorer and marginal students, you must draw upon the entire arsenal of motivational techniques I have referred to earlier. There are no absolutes or guaranteed methods. Letters home may do it for some students, especially weekly listings of home-work assignments, those up-coming as well as those not turned in. Pats on the back may do it for some others. "The Big Brother" approach, the drill sergeant, the contract -- all have merit. Here in lies the skill of the one-to-one motivator: recognition of the techniques that will hit home. Remember what Franklin Roosevelt once said, "Try something; if it doesn't work try something else, but above all, do something."

I stumbled upon a motivational idea in the middle of a school year some years back that proved literally exciting. Teaching a class of U.S. History students who did not seem to grasp the relationship between doing homework and passing the course, I put up a sheet of graph paper listing their names at the bottom and numbering from one to one hundred points running up the side of the paper. Since each of my homework assignments carried an assessed point value, it was easy to create a bar graph showing their progress toward one hundred points. Then, as I graded each set of papers I would inch their bar up the "Ladder of Academia," as I called it, by drawing each individual line with a felt-tip marker. The kids loved it. Their biggest problem was pronouncing "academia." Those who chose to remain at the bottom of the ladder did so of their own volition and it was apparent to all. The net result was an increase in the work performed by what had been a lack-luster class.

Carry this further -- what about the classified student who has real problems comprehending the work? Public shame and the posting of grades, as I have advocated, can be truly harmful. This student needs a helping hand, not a tongue-lashing. Some time-tested ideas come from a school psychologist I have been privileged to work with over the past few years, Clement S. Bramley. First of all, flexibility is critical in

dealing with the classified student. Vary your
techniques to whatever the troubled student can handle.
If he can only take tests orally, then give him oral
tests during a mutually free period. Ask him what he
feels most comfortable with. Secondly, give him as much
structure as possible -- notesheets, filmstrips, study
guides, reading guides, vocabulary lists. Third,
incorporate reinforcement, practice and drill into your
lessons. Go over his work with him right there,
correcting as you go. Repetitive drill helps the
classified student and gives him self-confidence. Even
rehearsal of questions prior to testing can be justified
and certainly does help. Consult with other teachers,
his parents and even peers, although tactfully with the
latter. Perhaps most importantly, give him praise.
This student knows that he has problems and is often
easily frustrated by failure. Pat him along the way,
build him up, and give him a sense of worth and success.
This student can be your most rewarding teaching
assignment.

     With any students who are experiencing long-term
academic difficulties, a low self-esteem begins to
surface. They begin to expect failures. It is your job
then, to have them meet with whatever successes you can
create. Scale down the difficulty of certain assignments or assign artwork in place of written work. This
is not to suggest that you become a teacher whose work
is child-like or easy, but rather this is meant to
convey the idea of flexibility and short-term success
motivation. These types of assignments are geared for
individual students too, not the entire class.

     We hear of the term "relating to students." What
does this mean and where does one draw the line?
Essentially, relating to students refers to the
enjoyment of working with kids day in and day out. This
is why we, as teachers, are different. Most adults like
to occasionally work with children; we must enjoy it as
a career. At one time, people entered the teaching
profession because it was considered a relatively "safe"
job (as long as there were children, there would be
teachers) and tenure meant little work/much security
once it was attained. This type of thinking has
absolutely no place in our profession. We are not paid
enough money for the job to be anything less than enjoyable. Thus, beginning with the premise of liking
children, the second step must be a desire to make them

better than you are. Do not be on an ego trip and do not hold back in your teaching and their development. It may seem at times that I derive my quotations at the beginning of each chapter from apparently unlikely sources, so let me offer this quote from a weight training instructor named Vince Gironda who said, "The true teacher hopes that his students surpass himself."

Do not feel threatened by an intellectual class. Admit your shortcomings to yourself, go out and do your homework preparing for the class lectures, and then enjoy the kids. As I have indicated before however, teach them differently than you teach your other classes. Allow them feedback and critical reflection on ideas.

Similarly, approach the poorer academic class in a different manner. Humor is a big factor here. You can relate to these students particularly with a street-wise ability to wisecrack and be able to handle the return crack. Be able to laugh at yourself -- I cannot emphasize this enough. It all boils down to the ego once again. The ego must be minimized when dealing with children. Enjoy your job. Show your concern. Do it with humor and humility, certainly not easy to master, but critical for the student-teacher relationship.

There is, however, a line of demarcation. Although I have been called "a big kid" because of my, at times, childlike enthusiasm, I would never allow myself to be "one of the kids." There is a very distinct difference. For one, do not join students in their social lives; consider this a taboo. You are the adult and they look up to you. Once they look down at you, or even parallel with you, respect diminishes. I think that the key factor here is in the area of decision-making. As long as you, not the children, make the key decisions, you are the boss and therefore are seen as on a higher plane of authority. Be sure that your decisions are based on rationality not emotion, fairness and not favoritism, objectivity and not an ill-considered attempt at acceptance. It is not important to have the students like you as a peer. Do not even strive for it, for if you were to be accepted on a peer basis, your professionalism would be finished. A particular decision may be unpopular, but you will not necessarily be unpopular for making it. Along the same lines, push for the big things that you deem important, not the trivialities. Let the students have some leeway. Your way may not always be the best way, but it is your job to draw the lines of parameter and perimeter.

Another aspect of motivation and relating to students is to let them know that academically you are one of them and you share their struggles; you can sympathize. Do not forget the days you spent as a student. If possible, continue your education beyond the undergraduate degree. By so doing, you remain mentally sharp and share an academic workload with your pupils. I said at the opening of this volume that it will definitely improve your teaching if you remain a student. Furthermore, you will not only be aware of innovations in your field, but you will find that the way you study now improves later as you experiment and change. Thus, you can forward this experimentation along to your students. I write papers differently now and study for tests differently now than I did as an undergraduate. Hopefully, my study skills and techniques have improved. One final point is relevant here and it comes from a police journal: "One of the best ways to prevent burn-out is through self-improvement." Always be a student.

What about using grades as a motivator? Every teacher, of course, has his own ideas on this, but it is fairly well accepted that grades should be used as a positive rather than a negative incentive. Never use a grade to punish a student. You must, even in a legal sense, give the student what he or she has numerically earned. You may choose not to give him or her that extra point up to a B, but you cannot give a grade below what is earned. You will leave yourself open for much difficulty in explaining such a grade.

Janice Gruendel, in a 1975 study by Cullen, reported that the use of grades as an incentive does work. When students were presented with a no-penalty situation for not submitting an assignment, in most cases nothing came in. But when a grade was attached to the assignment, the work was done. This finding is to a large degree common sense, but what most of us should consider is how we are to use late penalties as an incentive to get students to turn in work once it is past due. Many teachers feel that a full letter grade or a set pattern of point-reduction is best. However, I submit that once a student fails to bring in his work after three or four days in this scenario, he might as well forget it altogether because the penalty is so steep that it is not worth doing the assignment. Thus we both lose -- we cannot evaluate the student's work and the student does not learn from the lesson. I have suggested a diminishing late penalty approach. Offer steep penalties for the first and second days late, but taper off the assessment as the days go on. Why? Consider that it is always better for the educational process if the student has done the work than if he has not. By telling the student that he will get some credit for the work no matter how late, the incentive to perform is always there. Furthermore, I tell the students that unless the work is copied or grossly deficient, then I will never penalize for lateness down below 20 percent of the credit value of the work.

Involve parents. Incorporate them into your motivational plan. As noted before, I like to send home notes and memos about student work. You can carry this further with semester homework listings, course reading lists, and so on. Let the parents know exactly what their child will have to do by way of assignments. On the high school level, all too often inquisitive parents are met with "Yeah, my work's all done" or "We didn't have any homework tonight." How are the parents to know otherwise?

An intriguing federal study once found that with A-students, some 32 percent cited direct parental involvement in their schooling. With C-students, only 13 percent could say the same. Similarly, among the A-students, 67 percent mentioned that their parents met with or called teachers when they experienced academic difficulties; less than 50 percent of the C-students cited this.

Why not allow parents into you classroom during instructional time? Why not have parents sign contracts when they register their children for school? These would stipulate that the parents will work with the school in the Parent-Teacher Organization, office work, coaching, or speaking in classes. Why not send home "School Rules" such as time allocations for television viewing, mutual agreements on the serving of alcohol at parties, the time parties break up, and so on? Perhaps our schools are missing the boat by not sufficiently tapping parental resources. It is undeniably true that the most vibrant school systems are those that view the school as a community resource and not an isolated ivory tower.

Two other factors have to be considered in student motivation: the role of performance objectives and the concept of knowing your students. Performance objectives sound ominously "educational." All of us have written or seen behavioral objectives, performance objectives, task-orientation plans, behavioral goals and so on. Of course, it all amounts down to what we expect the student to do after a lesson is taught. However, let us translate this into practical classroom application. Tell the students what is demanded of them, what they have to do to pass, and then what is needed for excellent work. Be specific; let them know exactly what you want. Instead of assigning a book report of unspecified detail, tell them you want a book review containing 1000 words, bibliographical data, title page, summary of the book including the author's main point or thesis, a critical analysis of the work, and a concluding paragraph on how the book will help them in their study for this course. Again, be specific. Now if the student fails to do what is required, then he has made the decision to do sub-par work and he knows that he is incurring a penalty. I do not mean to imply that everything must be so cut and dried as to be fixed into objectivity, but try to make things as clear as possible and still retain a degree of subjectivity. Earlier I spoke of contracts; these are applications of performance objectives also.

Knowing your students. This is where we must all try to be psycho-analysts. Try to "read" your students. What pressures do they face? Are the students working to their potential? Do you trust them? Do you believe what they say? What is their homelife like? Who are their friends? How are they doing in other classes? What is their self-confidence level? What are their extra-curricular activities, hobbies, religious preferences? You need not be a detective here, but rather be perceptive. Inquire. Listen. The Faculty Room can be a breeding ground of rumors and discontent, but it can also provide some good insight into students if you enter with that as your objective. I have even had students fill out personal data sheets directly inquiring what some might consider "none of my business." Give kids the option to fill these out, however; you will find that most comply.

Once you have "read" the students, then try to develop diagnostic theories about each child and his or her performance. It will be gratifying and somewhat surprising to see how often you will be correct. Furthermore, do not be afraid, when dealing with parents, to espouse your theory about their child. Most will appreciate your professional assessment and candor. And then they may tell you that you are wrong and correct you, or you will have told them what they suspected all along. Either way the end result is a diagnostic evaluation of what makes up the child's psyche and personality. This obviously helps you in dealing with the child and knowing when to apply the boot in the butt or the pat on the back.

Before leaving this topic, I cannot help but relate an anecdote that I came across in a book by Thomas G. Devien entitled <u>Teaching Study Skills</u> (Allyn & Bacon, 1981). He cites Lowry (1961). It is the story of the mouse and Henry Carson and it says something to all of us.

One summer evening a mouse scampered through the offices of the Educational Testing Services and accidentally triggered a delicate mechanism just as the data for a student named Henry Carson was being scored.

Henry was an average high school student whose scores on the College Board were reflective of his mediocrity. The mouse caused the computer to misfire and the scores that registered for Henry became nothing less than remarkable -- 800 on both the verbal and math tests!

When these scores came back to Henry's school, the word spread like wildfire. Teachers re-assessed the hitherto unknown Henry. This must be a brilliant child. How could they have been so wrong? Guidance counselors scrambled back to the college guide. Henry's parents boasted of their new-found genius. Henry's friends stepped back aghast and then crowned him "a brain" in their midst.

But the biggest change came from within Henry himself. He was being treated so differently that he responded in a positive way. More thought and more

effort went into his work. He read more, spoke out
more, ran for student office. A kind of self-fulfilling
prophecy began to unfold. Henry excelled. Henry went
on to a top-ranking college and even graduated with
honors...

The obvious message here is that we must avoid
labeling students. Never tell a child that he will
never be able to do something or that he will never
amount to anything. Do not make predictions about his
or her future; just try to shape it in as positive a way
as you can.

Incredible as it seems, Louis Pasteur, Louisa May
Alcott, Richard E. Byrd, Walt Disney, Ludwig van
Beethoven, Albert Einstein, Isaac Newton, and F. W.
Woolworth were told that they would never make it in
their chosen fields! Leo Tolstoy, Winston Churchill,
and Werner Von Braun actually failed at some point in
their school careers!

PART VII

AFTERWORD

"If you do what you have been doing,
you will continue to get what you
have been getting."

Dr. Harry K. Wong

"There is only one evil among men --
ignorance; against this evil there is
only one medicine -- learning; but this
medicine must be taken not in homeopathic
doses, but by the pail and by the forty-
pail barrel."

Dmitry Pisarev, Russian
literary critic and 19th
century nihilist

Perhaps the most difficult aspect of writing any book is finishing it. Some writers may have problems completing their book; others have problems deciding when to conclude it and wrap it up. The latter has been my problem. Even as I send this manuscript to the editor, I can always remind myself of another angle, another point, or another way to phrase textual narrative that has already been written down.

As of this writing, this book has been eight years in the making. It has been eighteen years in creation as I have plowed, blundered, stumbled and, at times, hopefully succeeded in my teaching career. It is my earnest desire that others who may read this can benefit from my errors and not make them. Just as hopefully, the reader can take some of my "coaching points" and use them, either in whole or in part, in their classroom.

I must apologize for my citing of un-named studies at various points in the manuscript. Much of this information has been garnered from graduate classes, seminars, teacher in-service presentations and so forth. More often than not, the study was not named at the time the data were presented to me. Hence, I offer these findings as food for thought.

In conclusion, let me simply tie it all together with these reminders -- enjoy your students, have fun in your classroom, use a mixture of common sense, academia, and a healthy dose of humanity.

RMT

Manasquan, New Jersey

ABOUT THE AUTHOR

Richard M. Trimble is a teacher in the Manasquan, New Jersey school system where he was chosen as the district Teacher of The Year in 1982, 1983 and 1985. He holds a Bachelors Degree from the University of Bridgeport, a Masters Degree in History from Seton Hall University, an Associate Degree in Criminal Justice from Brookdale Community College and is currently working on his doctorate. Richard has taught on the faculties of William Paterson College and Brookdale Community College. He is the author of numerous articles on teaching and coaching and writes a weekly newspaper column. Mr. Trimble is married, the father of three, 41 years old, and still a classroom teacher.